POWER

and

WISDOM

The New Path For Women

Priscilla V. Marotta, Ph.D.

What successful women are saying about
Power and Wisdom: The New Path for Women.

"Dr. Marotta's book sheds positive new light on *power*, a word that is uncomfortable for many women. Marotta's redefinition allows us to see *power* as a life-enhancing skill to be developed."

—Carolyn Elman, Executive Director
The American Business Women's Association

"*Power and Wisdom: The New Path for Women* acts as a tool to build a strong inner foundation, one that can weather the many storms that will blow in during a lifetime. It opens the doors in our minds, my granddaughter's, her mother's, mine…to become more aware of our strengths and uniqueness, to recognize our needs and wants, and to evaluate where we are and where we are going. We need this book to help us balance our lives, strengthen our confidence, and prepare for the 21st Century."

—Sue I'lala'ole, CEO
www.womenonwallstreet.com

"An exceptional book, and right on point for today's woman!"

—Susan Sumrall, Deputy
Broward Sheriff's Office

"This is a critical subject for women working in traditionally male dominated fields. The issues you address in this book are essential for women to succeed and to be happy in their success. I intend to recommend it to my students and friends."

—Dr. Sheila E. Browne, Professor of Chemistry
Mount Holyoke College

"Who steals your authority, and who let's them? This book shows how you can stop the power thieves and be transformed into a powerful, generous, caring, feminist for the future."

—Penelope C. Paine
Gender Equity Consultant

"Traditional concepts of *power* bring to mind a loud, reckless motorboat contaminating the air and plowing over obstacles. In contrast, women can learn to use *power* much as a sailboat uses the *power* of the wind to reach its destination—quietly, considerate of its surroundings, beautifully, and yet with sweeping effectiveness!"

—**Amy Arnold, M.D.**
  Surgeon

"How handy to have a tidy list of Power Robbers. Just the clarity of seeing them in black and white makes them less ephemeral and easier to challenge. Then, a list that kicks one into the appropriate *power* place...It stirs the pot and enables one to develop personally designed *power*. There's no limit!"

—**Jackie Joseph, Actress**
  Board of Directors of The Screen Actors Guild

"You have given all women a useful glimpse into the sad fact that we are often the architects of our own glass ceilings. More important, you have shown us how to shatter it without cutting ourselves."

—**Pamela I. Perry, Attorney, Partner**
  Kenny Nachwalter Seymour Arnold Critchlow & Spector

"The real wonder is that a woman's entire universe can sometimes be kept under a Glass Ceiling; one which not only limits their earnings, but also blocks their view and sometimes keeps them from reaching for the stars."

—**Anita Perez Ferguson, President**
  National Women's Political Caucus

"Each of us as a woman is capable of yielding a phenomenal amount of *power*, but we need to be *taught* the skills in developing this *power* to achieve our goals and survive in the business world."

—**Linda E. Grabowski, President**
  Sisco, Inc.

"I encourage you to read this book not as an intellectual exercise but as a blueprint for taking control of your life."
—**Cathy Feldman, Editor/Publisher**
   Blue Point Books

"I must concur that Dr. Priscilla Marotta's depiction of contemporary women's negative attitudes toward feminism and *power* are very accurate as is her depiction of the Glass Ceiling. I typically encounter many students who have a very negative view of feminism and woman *power*. Dr. Marotta provides her reader with the psychological tools she needs to identify and plug her *power* drains and to develop her personal *power*, I am positive that *Power & Wisdom: The New Path for Women* will have an enormously empowering effect on the women who read it, especially those aspiring to leadership positions in business. I believe that the wealth of information and practical tools provided in this book will empower you to become a fully functioning, self-confident business woman."
—**Mary Zahm, Ph.D., Assistant Professor of Psychology**
   Bristol Community College

"When I accepted that my innately feminine responses and modes of behavior were valid, and "better," I became a far more effective and successful leader and my own emotional health was greatly benefited. I have been able to achieve in an industry (construction in NYC) that is predominantly male by being true to my feelings, sentiments and instincts. And I have a far greater understanding and appreciation of the *power* and potential within me, and all women."
—**Constance Cincotta, President**
   Brooklyn Mason Supply

"*Power* is my connection to the universe. Reminding myself of that connection allows me to move forward through life's ripples."

—**Linda B. Selleck**
   Massachusetts Educator

"*Power and Wisdom* can help at a personal level, it validates the fears women have about leadership and then provides a guide for them to cultivate the skills to take charge and move ahead."

—**Betty Shepperd, Director**
   HOSPICE

"I was delighted to see that a book on women and *power* has finally been written. As you stated, "*power*" has too often been perceived as a negative term and one that too few women can relate to…This is a wonderful time to be talking about *power* and abilities. For someone to succeed in the 21st century, he/she must coalesce all the best qualities of the best people. It will be the interconnectedness of people, ideas, and data that will create new stars to shine in corporations."

—**Susan Fenner, Ph.D., Manager**
   Education and Professional Development
   International Association of Administrative Professionals

"If you read no other book this year, read *Power and Wisdom!* This book will give you the skills to move beyond the Glass Ceiling and reach new heights. Learn to use your unique feminine abilities and wisdom to achieve a powerful presence for collaborating with powerful women and men."

—**Dr. Monica Querci**
   Physician

Printed in the United States of America
Book production by Phelps & Associates, Cover design by Knockout Design, Cover photograph by Elson Alexandre, Logo design by Luzmary Jiminez, Website design by Marcelo Paiva

Levenson, H. (1981). "Differentiating among internality, powerful others, and chance." H. Lefcourt (ed.), *Research with the locus of control construct*. New York: NY: Academic Press, 1, 15-59. Reprinted by permission of the author.
"Declaration of Sentiments - 1998." Reprinted by permission of the National Organization for Women.

Cataloging-in-Publication Data
(provided by Quality Books, Inc.)

Marotta, Priscilla.
      Power & wisdom: the new path for women/
      Priscilla V. Marotta – 1ˢᵗ ed.
      p. cm.
      Includes bibliographical references and index.
      ISBN: 0-9666339-0-3

        1. Businesswomen—United States—Psychology.
      2. Businesswomen—United States—Attitudes. 3.
      Self-esteem in women—United States. 4.
      Self-confidence—United States. I. Title.

    HQ1206.M37 1998   646.7'0082
              QBI98-1093

Names and identifying characteristics of the patient examples used for this publication have been altered. Any similarities of the names or characteristics of any living persons in the clinical case examples are purely coincidental and not intended by the author. This publication is designed to provide accurate and authoritative information in regard to the subject matter covered. It is sold with the understanding that the author or publisher are not engaged in rendering psychological, legal, or other professional services. If expert assistance is needed, the services of a competent professional should be sought.

Attention Corporations and Organizations

Copies of these books are available at special quantity discounts for bulk purchases, sales, promotions, premiums, corporate sales, education, or fund-raising use. Special books or book excerpts can be created to fit specific needs. Contact: Director of Special Markets Department, Women of Wisdom, Inc. 300 N.W. 70ᵗʰ Avenue, Suite 302, Plantation, FL 33317, Telephone: 1-877-WISDOM-7, Fax: (954) 583-9575 or 1-888-200-2424

On the Worldwide Web at: http://www.womenofwisdom.com

To my beloved, deceased mother, Fleurdelis Valerie Marotta:
She gave me permission to be powerful
and shared her love of literature.

To my beloved, deceased father, Joseph Francis Marotta:
He loved me and respected my feminist beliefs.

To my beloved, deceased godmother, Violanda DiVenuti:
She inspired me to treasure life and celebrated my talents.

To my beloved godfather, Lawrence DiVenuti:
He is a role model of intellectual discipline
and encourages my dreams.

To my husband, Robert MacDonald:
He challenges my thinking, supports my
multiple projects, and adds joy to my life.

To my son, Christopher Joseph Fiore Marotta:
He teaches me the wisdom of youth.

To my patients:
They invite me into their lives and give me an invaluable
window into the struggles of living.

About the author...

Nationally recognized psychologist, Priscilla V. Marotta, Ph.D., is an executive coach, therapist, professional speaker, trainer, and consultant. Her treatment philosophy is "solutions...not talk."© Her specialties include dual career couples, women's issues and trauma. She has been a featured guest on television, radio, and a columnist for the *Miami-Herald.*

Dr. Marotta has been the recipient of numerous awards including: Florida Psychological Association's *What a Woman Award* for her contributions to the psychology of women, Millennium Medal of Honor, International Who's Who of Professionals, The World's Who's Who of Women, Who's Who in Medicine and Healthcare, The International Who's Who of Professional & Business Women, The Twentieth Century Award for Achievement, and Two Thousand Notable American Women. Dr. Marotta is Director of the Center of Psychological Effectiveness, in Fort Lauderdale, Florida and President of Women of Wisdom, Inc. Women of Wisdom is a corporation dedicated to activating the positive power of women and facilitating collaboration between women and men.

To Contact the Author:

C.O.P.E.

Priscilla V. Marotta, Ph.D.
Licensed Psychologist - PY0003973

Depression ♦ Relationship Issues ♦ Trauma
Menopause ♦ Life Coaching ♦ Aging

Center of Psychological Effectiveness, Inc.
6950 Cypress Road, Suite 103A
Plantation, FL 33317-2360

(954) 583-8831 x: 300
(800) 714-COPE
FAX (954) 583-9575

drmarotta@solutionsnottalk.com
www.solutionsnottalk.com

TABLE OF CONTENTS

Foreword 12
Executive Profile, Pat Moran 13
Acknowledgments 15
Introduction 17

Chapter 1. Power Is Not a Dirty Word 21

Power & Women 23
Power – What Is It? 24
Power Is Feminine 27
Stigma of Power 30
Positive Power 32
Power As a Skill 32
Power As a Life Necessity 34
Positive Power and the Glass Ceiling 36
Powering-Up 37
Star Points 39

Chapter 2. Power Robbers 41

The Experience 43
How Power Robbers Develop 44
Acquiring Positive Power Skills 47
Female Stereotypes 49
Power Robber #1: If I am accommodating and pleasing,
   I will have many friends and a rewarding life. 53
Power Robber #2: I want to do it right and not
   make mistakes. 56
Power Robber #3: I obtain security in life by finding a
   suitable life partner. 60
Power Robber #4: I want to avoid upsetting others. 64
Power Robber #5: I need to be polite and not make
   direct requests. 68
Power Robber #6: I need to treat everyone equally. 72
Power Robber #7: I need to obey the rules. 75
Power Robber #8: If there is a problem, it is my fault. 78
Power Robber #9: I must keep the peace and not
   make waves. 81
Power Robber #10: I must wait to be recognized
   for my achievements. 84
Controlling Power Robbers 86
Who Controls Your Fate? 88
Star Points 92

Chapter 3. Positive Power Lessons 93

Power Lessons 95
Lesson #1: I need to set limits and engage in
    adequate self-care. 97
Lesson #2: I welcome mistakes as an indicator that
    I am pushing my limits and being all I can be. 102
Lesson #3: I create security by developing my own
    competencies. 105
Lesson #4: I seek the respect of others and recognize
    that some people will be uncomfortable around me. 108
Lesson #5: I need to ask for what I want to reach
    my goals. 111
Lesson #6: I need to be discriminating in my
    interactions with others. 114
Lesson #7: I need to understand the rules and
    be flexible. 117
Lesson #8: I need to engage in positive self-talk
    and monitor over-responsibility. 120
Lesson #9: I want to make waves and be a change
    catalyst. 124
Lesson #10: I acknowledge my accomplishments and
    seek appropriate recognition. 128
Activating the Lessons 130
Star Points 131

Chapter 4. Women Yesterday and Today 133

Why History Is Important 135
The First Wave of Feminism 137
The Second Wave of Feminism 140
The Third Wave of Feminism 147
The Glass Ceiling 151
Star Points 154

Chapter 5. Feminism Needs a Facelift 155

Distortions—Distortions 157
Anti-Male 159
The Dangers Of Gender Wars 162
Anti-Beauty 165
Anti-Family 167
Neuter 168
Women's Studies 170

Sisterhood 171
Women-to-Women: Change Catalysts 172
Beyond the Word 174
Star Points 177

Chapter 6. The Wisdom of Women 179

Self-Acknowledgment 181
Data Gatherers 183
Information Sharers 184
Flexibility 185
Power Sharers 186
Collaboration 186
Win-Win Negotiators 187
Multitask Wizards 188
Change Tolerant 189
Team Leadership 190
Innovators 191
Integrators 192
Tap Your Talents 192
Star Points 194

Chapter 7. Star Power 195

Creating Versus Waiting 197
Partnership Versus Adversaries 198
Support Versus Divisiveness 199
A Victory Parade 202
Moving Beyond 209
Star Points 211
Afterword 212
Executive Profile, Holly C. Giertz 216

Appendices:

A: Suggested Readings 217
B: One Hundred Networking Resources for Women 218
C: Fifty Empowering Websites 231

Resources & Bibliography 237

Deliver the Dream 250

Index 252

Foreword

The lives of women today represent a balancing act. Weighing the needs of the many areas of our lives is not an easy task, and we all seem to be searching for answers to help us achieve fulfillment and happiness. More women than ever before are climbing diverse career ladders and moving into leadership positions at work. At the same time, our families remain a tremendous priority and we spend a great deal of time and energy nurturing our children and worrying about the happiness of our significant others. Women may feel torn when choices are made, given the limited hours in the day. Our natural tendency to be "other-focused" is the reason women often feel pulled in many directions, and this book explores how these same feminine qualities also can be strengths in our daily lives.

The same qualities that make us "other-focused" enable us to be successful at juggling all of the diverse areas of our lives. We need to learn to appreciate our feminine qualities as strengths, and use them to our greatest advantage. Many advice books have been written for women that tell us we should suppress our femininity in order to be successful in business. These books have taught us that being a woman is a disadvantage, and that we should learn to act like men to be successful. We have been told not to show our nurturing side, to model our communication style according to how men talk with each other, and to never reveal our emotions or feelings.

This type of advice only creates additional stress for women and cannot be effective in guiding us toward reaching our career goals or any of our goals in life. When you ask women who have reached the top of the ladder how they got there, very few will tell you that it was because they behaved like men. I have always believed that women bring unique qualities to the business table, and these feminine qualities balance and enhance the knowledge and expertise of male colleagues.

I was very excited to hear about the premise of this book, because my own approach to business and management has always seemed to go against the grain of what the advice books were encouraging. Finally, women would have a guide that shows us how to use our own feminine power to the fullest potential.

I use the term "power" because that is another major component of this book. For women, that word usually has negative connotations. However, taken in its purest definition, power can be used in a non-masculine, non-aggressive and non-confrontational manner to achieve positive goals. We have to get beyond the idea that power is synonymous with masculinity.

This book will help you learn to harness and use your own positive power to reach your dreams. It reaffirms that we can be ourselves, and still be effective leaders in business. Finally, it helps us remember to take care of ourselves, even as we are nurturing others.

Pat Moran
President/CEO
JM Family Enterprises, Inc.

Executive Profile, Pat Moran

Pat Moran is President and CEO of JM Family Enterprises, Inc., and President of its core company, Southeast Toyota Distributors, Inc., the world's largest Toyota distributor. She is dealer/principal of Margate, Florida-based JM Lexus, the largest volume Lexus dealer in the world. JM Family was listed as the 22nd largest privately owned company in the United States, according to most recent ranking. The company has major operations in Deerfield Beach, Florida; Jacksonville, Florida; Mobile, Alabama and St. Louis, Missouri.

She joined JM Family 15 years ago, and held a variety of positions including Vice President of Associate Relations, where she was responsible for managing Human Resources activities for JM Family; and Group Vice President of Sales, where she directed the marketing and dealer organizational activities for Southeast Toyota. Pat joined JM Family in an entry-level position as a clerk, and rose through the ranks gaining on-the-job training, and learning the business firsthand through each position she held.

Since 1989, Pat has served as President and CEO. Under her direction, JM Family Enterprises, Inc., has consistently surpassed sales and customer satisfaction objectives to maintain its position as an industry leader. Since she became President, JM Family's revenues grew from $2.4 billion to a projected $6.1 billion in 1998. She has also successfully managed JM Family's growth into new automotive-related businesses as well as expansion in core businesses.

Pat is actively involved in several organizations that are dedicated to helping abused and disadvantaged children. Most recently, she has become involved in Take Stock in Children, a program that provides mentoring and scholarships to disadvantaged high school students. In addition, she is a recipient of the Excalibur Award from the American Cancer Society for her lead role in the Breast Cancer Initiative, a program developed by the American Cancer Society to increase awareness of the importance of early breast cancer detection.

Pat is an active member of the Committee 200, a national organization of women business leaders, the National Association of Automobile Dealers (NADA), and the American International Automobile Dealer Association (AIADA). She is on the Board of Directors of Take Stock in Children, American Heritage Life Insurance and Boca Raton Resort and Club. She recently was inducted into the Florida Council of 100.

Pat is a recipient of Northwood University's Distinguished Women of the Year Award, Leadership Broward's Leader of the Year Award and the National Mother's Day Committee's Outstanding Mother Award.

She attended Marquette University in Chicago, her native city. She has three children and four grandchildren.

Acknowledgments

In the course of my life, many inspirational people have graced my path. My heartfelt thanks to my friends, professors, networking women, family, and the patients who have been an inspiration for this book.

My very special thanks to my original Massachusetts women's group who encouraged me to receive my doctoral degree. This group initiated my participation in the Second Wave of feminism. It is only fitting that this book is being published following the twenty-first anniversary of our group. The members of the group in alphabetical order are: Nancy Hallen, who mobilized to receive her MBA degree; Leona Ittleman, Esquire, a community leader, attorney, business dean, and early corporate challenger; Sharon Grover-Renda, my close soul mate, who has made a transition from educator to corporate executive; Linda Selleck, who maintained her commitment to education, and always kept the group in touch; and Suzanne Wallace, an educator, IBM corporate survivor, and community leader for the Big Brothers/Big Sisters Program. The Boston group was a significant catalyst for the achievements of our members.

Carolyn Thornton-Nation, an exceptional romance and travel writer, inspired my doctoral studies journey from Miami to Mississippi and has been an ongoing colleague. My major doctoral Professor, James Hollandsworth, Ph.D., helped me hone my writing skills, and inspired me in my entrepreneurial endeavors. Ginger Burks, RN, was a supportive advocate for my dissertation research, and friend. Ellen Schloss, Barbara Koffler, Myrna Ziegler, Psy.D., and Beth Arias have been consistent supporters. Debo Kotun, author, has been a resource and support. Additionally, Kathy Geller-Chen has been a close friend from my early doctoral days to the present, and helped brainstorm many of the concepts in this book. Additionally, Thomas Chen—who is fondly termed "my bro"—has been a significant emotional support.

Debbie Chase and Debra Moore, the administrative staff at the Center for Psychological Effectiveness, have been valuable management partners, and significant cheerleaders for my endeavors. Also, Tracy Boger tirelessly transcribed the book and was an invaluable resource. Technical assistance has been gratefully received from Tania Cowling, Donna Duffin-Ibrahim, Rosie Grupp, Wendy Forman, Gail Kearns, Caz Norwich, Penelope Paine, Janice Phelps, Peri Poloni, Dan Poynter, and Susan Warner.

My colleagues at the Center—Lauren Cohn, Ph.D.; Felicia Tralongo, Psy.D.; Faith Grobman, Psy.D; Sandi Khani, LMFT; Giselle Leibovitch, Ph.D.; Cristen Harris, MS, LD; and Donna Vignola, LCSW—have encouraged my journalistic efforts and shared their insights.

The South Florida Women of Wisdom Power Breakfast Group, which began in September of 1997 and continues monthly, was a focus group for the contents of the book. Moreover, many of these women's stories are intricately woven into the chapters of this book. The women of the Women Power Breakfast Group are: Amy Arnold, M.D., Surgeon; Darran Blake, Vice-President, Smith Barney, Inc.; Laurie Gordon-Brown, D.M.D., Dentist; Holly C. Giertz, Vice President of JM&A Group, a JM Family Enterprises, Inc. Company; Linda Grabowski, Printing and Graphic Arts Entrepreneur; Christine Lambertus, Esquire, Estates and Trusts Attorney; Andrea Lettman, Administrator, Foundation for Advanced Eye Care; Heidi Richards, Author, President of Eden Florist, and Founder, Women's Chamber of Commerce of Broward County; Carol Rudd, Real Estate Broker and Owner; Terry Santini, Former Vice Mayor of Davie and CPA; and Liana Silsby, Esquire, Trial Attorney. These eleven women have contributed not only their own ideas, but also their own experiences, enhancing the richness of the book. The personal stories of these dynamic women reflect the paradigm shifts needed for the new millennium.

The hundreds of women who have received treatment at the Center of Psychological Effectiveness were catalysts for my conceptualization of power skills in women's lives. The case studies cited in this book have been altered to protect their privacy. The principles of this book were developed through their journeys to positive power.

My brother, Joseph Marotta, my sister-in-law, Roberta Marotta, my cousin, Francesca Marchese, her spouse, John Marchese, and my dear friends, Anne and Ron Moscato, have been special champions in my life.

Introduction

Over the past forty years, women have experienced a widening of opportunities through new roles. American women have been positioned to move beyond the concerns of daily survival, and now possess both expanded opportunities and multiple demonstrated accomplishments. These achievements, as with all successes in life, extract a price. Women must learn positive power behaviors to keep the price affordable. Moreover, women need to ensure that their new successes do not cause overload, impeding their ongoing growth.

American women have become trailblazers in the expansion of life's options, experiencing lives of multiplicity, not simplicity. The expansion of women's lives necessitates, now more than ever, the increased utilization of power. Yet the concept of power still carries negative connotations for women who need to utilize power with increased comfort. As a woman who went back to college to obtain a doctorate at age thirty-five and became pregnant at forty, I personify a woman juggling many roles and creating new directions. Add to this picture that I own my own business, and multiplicity is evident.

As I assist the executive women who have come to me for help, it is clear that external achievements do not eradicate internal turmoil. Women are biologically programmed for nurturing-other behaviors, and such nurturing creates a propensity for overdoing, over-responsibility, and, subsequently, overload. When a woman attempts to moderate these behaviors to improve self-care and activate power, she experiences a level of discomfort, which complicates her attempt to balance a multifaceted life.

The physiological underpinnings of gender differences, which ensured survival of the species for millennia, do not necessarily support or match life choices in the 1990s. Specifically, women have a biological map to provide adequate care for offspring, producing an "other-directed" inner program. Focusing on the needs of others complicates a woman's ability to use power, for she tends to worry about people around her. Women appear to recoil from the word power, reacting as though they are being asked to give up their sense of self. Somehow, in the female vocabulary, power has taken on a problematic negative connotation. Transforming the negative label into a positive power mindset is a major challenge for women of the 1990s and the new millennium.

Feminine Wisdom

Many books give women tips on how to survive in the male world of business, but business is no longer validly and exclusively a male world. Women trailblazers of the next decade will thoughtfully utilize positive power, which in turn will increase their effectiveness in life and foster adequate self-care. Today, women are forty-six percent (46%) of the workforce and an integral part of the business world. Women-owned businesses employ one out of five United States workers and are over one-third of all companies. Other books have focused on male behaviors in power acquisition and use. In contrast, this book focuses on female behaviors from an updated view of women's power position in business and society. Women will be urged to use "feminine wisdom" to positively affect their lives, businesses, and society.

Feminine wisdom recognizes power as a necessary tool for effective living, and not solely for use by men. Power needs to stand as an independent, less emotionally laden word, describing effective political and social behaviors in the career-world and home-world. This book is intended for women seeking to:

1. become desensitized to the word power;
2. understand the concept of positive power;
3. develop an understanding of unique female issues involving power;
4. recognize the essential role of power in effective living;
5. dispel gender myths that create artificial barriers for women;
6. increase the range of feminine positive power tools for the new millennium;
7. mobilize women to increase recognition of their power position in society;
8. facilitate women to move beyond the Glass Ceiling to positions of societal change agents;
9. facilitate the feminist movement of the Third Wave, encouraging an effective collaboration of men and women for the new millennium; and
10. encourage women to lead a transformation of business and society.

What This Book Will Do For You

This book will demonstrate that power is not a dirty word! Power-training has been slighted in the cultural upbringing of many women, and the goal of this book is to introduce power-training concepts. Women readers will be encouraged to celebrate their unique talents, and join with me on a positive power journey. Male readers will increase their appreciation of the unique talents women bring to the workplace.

1

Power Is Not a Dirty Word

"Power is strength and the ability to see your-self through your own eyes and not through the eyes of another. It is being able to place a circle of power at your own feet and not take power from someone else's circle."

—*Lynn V. Andrews, Author*

Power & Women

Power and women—the phrase rings strangely in our ears. Powerful people have mainly been men. Throughout the centuries, women have been characterized as being weak, passive, and dependent—at the opposite end of the spectrum from the aggressive strengths attributed to men. Yet you do a disservice to both women and men by conceptualizing men as powerful, and strong at one end of the continuum while placing women at the opposite end of the continuum as passive and weak. To live a psychologically healthy life, men need to be able to express their feelings, demonstrate caring, and display some vulnerability. On the other hand, women need to exert leadership, mobilize to meet their needs, and manage their lives.

Multiple research studies show that gender characteristics are largely reflective of socialization patterns. As women and men grow up in a culture, multiple messages are communicated on female and male behaviors. The messages for women in United States society have been to be accommodating, deferential, nurturing, and demure. Only now are messages beginning to communicate women's utilization of power. Naomi Wolf discussed in *Fire with Fire* the need for women to be resocialized to recognize and use their power. Wolf notes that women have enormous unclaimed power, and states, "Women are far more powerful than they know, have far more leverage than they are using, and can raise their voices to make rapid, sweeping, irrefutable changes in the conditions of their lives."

Clearly, in both psychological research and mainstream literature, a momentum is building for women to be resocialized with a new set of power tools. This book is a resocialization manual for women to acquire power tools in their life, but differs from other perspectives by encouraging women to create a new perception of power. As a concept, power often becomes confused with control, and has been misused and distorted over the years. Dr. Offerman in *Psychology of Women Quarterly* noted, "Models of female achievement need to be more complex than models of male achievement, because women leaders reflect a blending of the traditionally male achievement profile with the uniquely female perspective."

You will see that power is a skill, like any other, for achieving goals. To be effective, women have to use power to put their beliefs and their needs into workable operation. Women clearly need the power to advance their own development, but they do not desire to use their power to limit the development of others. Women are challenged, as they enter the new millennium, to shed their lifelong conditioning that power is to be avoided. You need to jettison this belief, and move to an understanding of power as essential to effective living. Power pervades every aspect of our life, and is a creative force to be embraced. As you go forward in this chapter, women need to be prepared to have an open mind and a readiness to acquire power skills.

Power – What Is It?

Power is a word that has multiple meanings. Unfortunately, many of the meanings of power are shaded by images of domination and hurtfulness. Power has been contaminated by negative images of bulldozing or controlling others. The positive use of power requires one to separate the concept of power from the contamination of societal meanings. You cannot integrate power into your life without first wiping your minds clear of any preconceived ideas of power. But how do you start? The following exercise will enable you to identify your "power blocks." Take a few minutes and sit down with a blank piece of paper. Write the word **POWER** in large letters. Next, write down all of the words, feelings, and phrases you associate with power. This exercise will enable you to identify your "power blocks." Those words occurring to you that appear negative are your personal "power blocks."

Imagine for a moment that you are hearing the word power for the first time. Open your mind and your heart to understanding the concept of power from a perspective that you have never before held. Power requires increased study and understanding due to the lack of consistent definition. Furthermore, psychologists often talk about the power process without using the word power, and often have obscured the role of power skills in our lives.

Webster's Unabridged Dictionary has thirty-two definitions of the word power. *Webster* states that power is the "ability to do or act; capability of doing or accomplishing something, . . . great or marked ability to do or act; strength; might; . . . a person or thing that possesses or exercises authority or influence, . . . energy, force, or momentum, . . . to inspire; spur; sustain." Power is the ability to achieve. Power is the ability to expend energy, the force for bringing inspiration to others, and is central to being effective in life. Power is the key to personal achievement. One cannot be effective in life unless one is powerful.

Power is also a necessary part of living. Acting with confidence, having control over your life—this is use of power and it exists whenever two people interact in any setting. Power is not merely physical strength or force, such as with strong draft horses or other massive creatures. Power is different in humans with our unique ability to think and communicate. Power is the energy you emit to achieve goals in your life. Moreover, love has often been defined as the exchange of personal power to enhance the well-being of both individuals. An important mind shift for women may be to see power as the foundation of healthy love. Power use increases your "love quotient." For years, women have feared that to be powerful was to be "unlovable!" The opposite is the reality. A powerful you has thoughts, feelings, and accomplishments to share.

Being a powerful person not only enhances your love life; it enables you to survive. Power is very reassuring to the conscious human mind. Activation of power releases endorphins into the body system. The release of endorphins is essential to mental health, and a sound immune system, to maintain physical health. Several studies have demonstrated that the use of personal power has a positive influence on the health of the body. Research studies report that sixty percent (60%) of visits to physicians are by the "worried well." The relationship between psychological factors and physical health have been demonstrated in heart disease, gastrointestinal difficulties, cancer, and other diseases; this relationship even extends to studies on the rate of aging. A case can be made that power utilization enhances longevity. Thus, power is the mind's immune system for healthy living.

Exerting your power in romantic relationships is crucial to the health of the relationship. The four cornerstones of a healthy, romantic relationship are communication, respect, trust, and compatible sexual interactions. Effective respect, trust, and communication comes from your lover viewing you as someone who is capable and competent. Acquiring skills of capability and competency require the use of personal power. Inadequate use of personal power can undermine a romantic relationship. The following clinical case provides an example of power anorexia eroding a marriage. Power anorexia is the inability to use power.

Julie's Story

Julie was an attractive woman—thirty-four, tall, well-groomed—and employed in a managerial position for a national company. She sought therapy after her second divorce. During initial sessions, Julie was tearful, had difficulty expressing her feelings, and felt abandoned by both former spouses. Her husbands had been well-educated men, with financially stable jobs, and had been initially loving and caring in the relationship. During therapy sessions, a clear pattern began to emerge. Julie was an insecure woman who questioned her self-worth, needed a great deal of reassurance, and had constantly questioned her former spouses on their commitment to the relationship. Her last husband was still maintaining contact with Julie, and agreed to attend a session.

During the session, her former spouse, Tom, discussed at length his initial love and commitment to Julie. Tom shared that he had been worn down by Julie's childlike behaviors over their six-year marriage, and her need for constant attention and reassurance. He had reached the conclusion that Julie was unable to be a life partner. Tom stated, "In my future relationships, I need a woman who is in touch with her personal strengths and is able to be a powerful person, able to be a partner." Julie's case demonstrates that having a strong sense of your self-worth, clearly communicating your needs, and being a person who uses power allows mutual respect, mutual trust, and a partnership relationship. Powerful behaviors enhance romantic attractiveness—contrary to the archaic myth that weakness adds to the attractiveness of the female. In actuality, personal strength and power increases romantic allure for women and men alike.

Power Is Feminine

Power is the ability to take action and engage in effective living. Neither men nor women own power. As the human species evolved, men were associated with physical power in their role as warriors seeking food. This beginning survival necessity of using male physical strength caused power to be associated with men. Yet physical power is a very small dimension of the concept of power. Even in the dictionary definition of power, physical powers ranks far down the list, appearing as *Webster's* fifteenth sub-definition.

Placing the physical powers of men in the proper perspective, one then moves to the whole phenomena of androcentrism. As Western civilization evolved, male behaviors became the benchmarks for desirable social behaviors. This social phenomena of male behaviors viewed as the "ideal" and female behaviors as the "other" is called androcentrism. This separation has been a limitation for individuals and society. Male and female behaviors are both valuable and essential to society and quality of life. Also, individuals cannot be explained or defined solely by their gender. You encompass a unique combination of skills, talents, and behaviors. Unfortunately, history, theory, and popular conceptions about power have not included or addressed women's experiences.

The assertiveness movement packaged a program to women that avoided a direct power-training program. Assertiveness training encouraged women to express their needs and be more vocal—to assert themselves. However, rather than foster woman empowerment, the subtle message was for women to "be appropriate" and "nice" in their expression of their new skills. Once again, women were deterred from being powerful. Now and in the new millennium, women need to understand and redefine power, not be excluded or discouraged from power use by verbal semantics.

Early in Western civilization, social stereotypes of women and men emerge. The difficulty with all stereotypes is that polarity thinking arises. Polarity thinking is black or white, and all-or-nothing thinking. It assumes the presence of opposites. In reality, human beings operate on a continuum. A continuum of behaviors exists with opposites being useful only as the contrast points. Few human beings exist at one or the other end of the spectrum. The majority of human beings are found somewhere on the continuum between the two points. Thus, polarity thinking does a disservice to both men and women. However, gender stereotypes and polarity thinking are still present today. The power stereotype is that men are powerful and women are weak, men are active and women are passive.

Often, women, as they consider power behaviors, find it difficult to overcome past stereotypic images. Thinking is a complex process with which we make sense of information that surrounds us, by imposing some mental order on it. Breaking stereotypes means reconsidering the mental order you've assigned. The cognitive framework or schema that one places around a concept is essential, and for a stereotype to be modified, new ideas have to be learned for the power concept. Problematically, highly valued feminine traits are warmth, expressiveness, peace-making, giving, nurturing, thoughtful, accommodating, emotional, and gentle. Although women possess these traits, it does not preclude them from using these traits with power. Power no longer can be only in the framework of male behavior. Power, as a cognitive framework, needs to be also incorporated into the female mindset.

Regardless of achievements, many women still squirm at the mention of power, yet most women are drawn to the concept. As I field tested the concepts for this book, the response to invitations for selected South Florida Professional Women to join a Women of Wisdom Power Breakfast Group was one hundred percent (100%) acceptance. In order to have the group be an intense, power-generating, brainstorming collective versus a networking collective, the group was closed to new members after it was formed, and remained limited in size. Once the word was out about the group, multiple requests were made to join. Clearly, women of achievement are aware of their needs for power-training. Yet, out of this achieving group of attorneys, doctors, and businesswomen, one asked, "Can we take the word power out of the title?"

This woman, who has many power behaviors, avoided the power term. Despite a strong maternal role model, she has ambivalent feelings about power. In her viewpoint, power is an uncomfortable word. She views power as something that is forceful and abrasive. Nonetheless, her behaviors in the group demonstrate that despite her discomfort with the word, she utilizes power effectively. She is comfortable with expressing her opinions, and different perspectives. She projects self-confidence and maintains appropriate self-care behaviors with exercise and health. She is an attractive and thoughtful woman who has multiple accomplishments. Yet with all of her demonstrations of power use, she does not want to be viewed as powerful. She believes the myth that power usage involves a lack of consideration for others, when in actuality power and consideration can go hand-in-hand. The sad reality is that ill-used power in the hands of some has given power "a bad name."

The dilemma of the negative connotations of power creates a double bind for many women. Even though women may yield power effectively, women are not comfortable with power. This creates an internal conflict which can limit your effectiveness. Limitations in life are something to be removed. Thus, you not only engage in powerful behaviors, you must be able to have internal comfort with the use of power. The Women of Wisdom Power Breakfast Group member, on some level, must have recognized the need to go to the next step. Her interest in joining the group, knowing that it was for powerful women, demonstrated her commitment to power. However, she experiences ongoing turmoil and difficulty reconciling herself to power usage. The editor of the book *at your core*, an anthology of women writing about power stated, "From these sources, I learned that many women (far too many) do not feel powerful in their personal lives."

Comfort with power begins with understanding the power you use daily. When you establish goals for your family, for yourself, or for your business, you are exercising power. Managing daily activities, activating decision-making, developing plans—all are exercises of power. When you conduct discussions with an employee or a colleague and brainstorm more effective ways of approaching a problem, you are being powerful. When men and women are in loving relationships with mutual reciprocity, they are expressing their personal power to each other. Power is integral to every moment of every day, and is to be treasured, not avoided. Power enhances femininity as a nurturing force creating internal strength and calm, and propels you toward effective living.

Stigma of Power

Power, unfortunately, has taken on connotations, far afield from its real meaning. A powerful person is seen as someone who dominates or controls others with inappropriate use of force. A powerful person has been viewed as one who may be controlling or manipulative, enslaves others, or is a user of people for selfish means. Power has been viewed in a hierarchical way of power-over others, rather than a power-with others. The dominant controlling version of power is power-over. This is the negative end of the continuum. The positive point of the continuum is power-with. Power-with promotes the well-being of self and others, and is inspirational and considerate of others.

Negative Power	Positive Power
Domination =	Inspiration =
Power-over	Power-with

Controlling behaviors have the goal of dominating others and generating negativity and adding stress to others. When power is utilized as power-over, it creates oppressiveness and victimizes other people. Controlling behaviors increase suffering and worry, and create fear. Controlling behaviors are the hallmark of the insecure individual that needs to dominate others for their own self-aggrandizement. The stigma of power arises from the confusion of power and control. *Webster* defines control as "to exercise restraint or direction over; dominate; command; to hold and check; curb." Control is the word that embodies dominating others. Control and power can often be confused in your mind. Power is effectiveness, confidence, and, the ability to achieve, but it is not control.

You must recognize that control is a separate word and concept. Unlinking the concept of control from the concept of power is essential for women. Power and control are separate words, separate concepts, and separate constellations of human behavior. Women's ability to incorporate power behaviors will be fast-forwarded when they remove the concept of control from the concept of power. Women need to engage in "out-of-the-box" thinking and reframe power as effectiveness. Dr. Lynn Offerman, developer of the Power Apprehension Scale (PAS), found that negative attitudes toward power will impact the types of influence strategies you use. If you view power negatively, you are at a high risk of limiting your ability to resolve problems. In the words of Congresswoman Corrine Brown, "Power is the ability to get things done, to make things better...." The term "positive power" will be used to facilitate the new cognitive framework of power independent from control.

Positive Power

Positive power is the ability to implement adequate life strategies. Positive power is power-with. Positive power allows an individual to be effective, to manage fears, to activate their energies, and to act with confidence. In order to facilitate a new non-aversive cognitive attitude, power independent of control will be termed positive power. Positive power includes powerful initiatives coupled with compassion.

POWER REDEFINED

Incorrect	Correct
➤ Force Used	➤ Peaceful Vision
➤ Control of Others	➤ Control of Self
➤ Oppression	➤ Liberation
➤ Adds Stress	➤ Manages Stress
➤ Causes Worry	➤ Eliminates Worry
➤ Generates Negativity	➤ Generates Positivity
➤ Stifles Creativity	➤ Sparks Creativity
➤ Creates Fear	➤ Limits Fear
➤ Limits Personal Growth	➤ Fosters Personal Growth

Power As a Skill

A person develops power by learning a range of life strategies. Power is not a genetic component, nor is it an elusive gem that you have to be lucky to unearth. Power is a skill to develop and expand throughout your life. Women need to engage in a new mindset to be able to acquire the skill with greater ease. The new mindset is transformational thinking. *The Last Word on Power* states "TRANSFORMATION is a function of altering the way you are *being*—to create something that is currently not possible in your reality." Thus, redefining power allows you to activate power.

The key to developing the positive power skills is to focus on the pronoun "I." Recognizing that "I" can only control self, reveals that "I" is the power trigger to move forward. As you focus on the "I" in your life, it is essential to recognize your strengths and to celebrate those strengths with an inner calm that generates a special charisma. Focusing on your "I" will allow you to assume a personal responsibility that is a catalyst to activating initiatives. The "I" focus is the ability to be proactive in your life. You still want to be considerate and thoughtful to others. The assumption of personal responsibility and the ability to create direction in your life are essential ingredients. You remain a nurturing woman who refuses to be emotionally hooked by your environment. You avoid emotional hooks by using positive power tools.

Angela's Story

Emotional hooks are important to avoid, as the clinical case of Angela demonstrates. Angela entered therapy as a thirty-two-year-old, attractive, married, retail executive with one preschool-age child. Angela was referred to therapy by her primary physician due to panic attacks that caused her to be fearful while driving. When she experienced a panic attack, her heart beat rapidly, a lump rose in her throat, her hands perspired, and she felt a constriction in her chest.

Angela was a community leader, involved with several charitable organizations. As therapy progressed, it became evident that Angela was a people-pleaser, and had difficulty setting limits with her staff, her colleagues, her friends, and her family. She would respond to requests with an affirmative answer without any consideration of other demands on her time. Angela was a classic case of a panic attack patient whose body was getting her attention due to her overdoing behaviors. During therapy, Angela learned a range of limit-setting skills and began to learn the skill of not responding to requests immediately. Angela also learned to carefully evaluate all requests. A prime example was an issue with her administrative staff. Angela was discussing in therapy how she appreciated her administrative staff staying late to help Angela with work. On further discussion, a review of job responsibilities uncovered that her assistant was not tending to her tasks in the workday. Angela was, in fact, staying after hours to help her assistant complete tasks which needed to be completed during the day.

Once she stepped back from the situation and realized that she was emotionally hooked by her assistant's inefficiency, a chain of events ensued. Angela went back to her place of employment, addressed the job description of the administrative assistant, held a job review with her and discovered that the assistant was spending excessive office time on personal phone calls rather than the needed work. Angela's panic attacks began to decrease dramatically as her administrative assistant appropriately assumed responsibility for her own work. Once Angela was able to clearly understand and identify her "I" needs and not be hooked by the many demands that were given to her, Angela's panic attacks were gradually eliminated. Thus, Angela is an example of a woman who learned new positive power skills, and implemented those skills with a positive impact on both her mental and physical well-being.

Power As a Life Necessity

Think for a moment. If you are not powerful, you are powerless. Like being in a boat without a rudder, powerlessness tosses you to and fro in the ocean of life. Unable to create a clear direction in your life, you ride the waves of daily living in an unfocused manner, ricocheting through life. Without the focus of positive power, your ability to be effective is at the whim of other individuals. You are a woman not in control; you are an ineffective human being.

Powerful behaviors generate positive perceptions, positive emotions, positive thoughts, positive words, positive attitudes, and proactive actions. Empowered women possess multiple strategies, decreased depression, and reduced anxiety. At the same time, interpersonal skills improve as you become more empowered, and more comfortable and adept at working with others. As you grow in positive power, you become an effective member of family and work teams, and your feeling of well-being allows you to be empathetic and compassionate to others. Also, as a powerful person, you generate a charisma and a positive aura that attracts others. As you develop your positive power skills, you will notice the effects quickly. As positive power skills become more and more integrated into your behaviors, you will feel calmer and more centered, maximizing your well-being. Positive power is essential to effective living, essential to your physical and mental well-being, and essential to your quality of life. A life without positive power is a life unlived. In the new millennium, the message to women is, "power-up."

Maryanne's Story

Lack of power can be expressed in many ways. Maryanne is an example of a woman rendered ineffective by a fear of making mistakes. Fears of being wrong can cause a power drain leading to powerlessness. Maryanne entered my office in tears. She was a woman in her early forties, and married with two teenage children. Maryanne was a college graduate who was experiencing extreme job stress, moving through six jobs in five years. Maryanne reported disruptive sleep, depressed mood, and feeling overwhelmed. She stated, "I have trouble making decisions, I am afraid of being wrong." Her fear of making mistakes was causing her to have a job paralysis that led to job dismissal after job dismissal.

During treatment sessions, Maryanne was able to reframe mistakes as an opportunity for learning. Additionally, Maryanne was able to focus on the value of taking initiative and mistakes were normalized as part of the learning curve of a new job. Just prior to the end of therapy, Maryanne received a raise and a promotion at her present job. Maryanne's ability to develop risk-taking skills and decrease her fears of making mistakes resulted in increased initiative and allowed her skills to be displayed more appropriately on the job. As Maryanne learned the power skills of initiative and risk-taking, she became an effective and valued employee and a significantly less distressed woman.

Positive Power and the Glass Ceiling

The acquisition of positive power skills is essential to moving beyond the Glass Ceiling, a term first coined in a *Wall Street Journal* article on March 24, 1986, and used to represent the artificial barrier which prevents qualified women and minorities from advancing into top level management positions. This journalistic phrase captures a wide range of behaviors into a succinct and descriptive term. The Glass Ceiling, like any artificial barrier, robs the organization of the talent of all employees. Whether the organization is government, education, business or a non-profit entity, limiting the talents of the staff negatively impacts productivity and stops the organization from realizing its full potential.

The Glass Ceiling Commission was established on November 21, 1991, as part of the Civil Rights Act of 1991. The Department of Labor recognized the need to eliminate barriers to the advancement of women and minorities. The vision of the Glass Ceiling Commission was to foster an enlightenment of national corporate leadership to recognize management diversity is a prerequisite for the long-term success of the United States in the domestic and global market. Four years later, the formal recommendations of the Federal Glass Ceiling Commission were released. The report's title *A Solid Investment; Making Full Use of the National Human Capital* aptly reflects the Commission's findings that companies who promoted women and minority workers had a higher growth rate than companies with rigid Glass Ceilings. Utilizing the talents of all employees translates to a positive impact to the "bottomline."

Multiple books and articles discuss strategies to move beyond the Glass Ceiling. Many of the strategies involve aggressive behaviors that "break through the Glass Ceiling" or "crash through the Glass Ceiling," as if it could be shattered by force. The key to the removal of the Glass Ceiling is for you to activate your unique wisdom as a woman. Few women want to mimic men and engage in dominating or controlling behaviors or become untrue to their essential nature. Rather, women want to use their unique abilities and sensitivities to move beyond the Glass Ceiling and remove it from consideration. The Glass Ceiling will no longer be a factor when women have wisely embraced positive power concepts.

Moving beyond the Glass Ceiling requires an activation of positive power tools. As your positive power tools are activated, you are able to advocate the acceptance of diverse viewpoints and opinions, and incorporate these diverse insights into policy. Diversity in the workplace needs to go beyond the diverse genders and ethnic backgrounds of employees. Diversity in the workplace needs to incorporate diverse viewpoints into policy.

Powering-Up

Throughout research and preparation for this book, personal, collegial, and clinical experience with hundreds of talented women convinced me of the importance to foster women's perception of themselves as powerful, talented, and valuable human beings. This is *not*, I emphasize, advocating for women to be male-like. Power can be expressed in multiple ways. The positive power that is essential to life is a calming power of personal clarity. The nurturing biological template for women gives rise to the potential for you, once you are in touch with your positive power, to reshape the world. There is not a single vision to be fulfilled in this reshaping. There is a vast multitude of possibilities to fulfill your individual vision. Women shall be like talented sculptors, uniquely shaping and guiding, contributing to the entire picture. Every woman will need to activate her positive power to assist the fluid, ongoing process of reshaping and creating a new sculpted paradigm. Every woman will need to activate her positive power, to be all that she can be, for to do less is to shirk from her responsibility to herself and her responsibility to the world at large.

As I foster the increased activation of positive power and pursue interlacing the power with wisdom for use by women, I recognized that you will continue to be challenged by your own use of power, for even positive power needs to be exercised with discretion and exceptional wisdom. The ambivalent feelings that women experience in relation to power stems from their keen appreciation of the responsibilities of power. I have great confidence in the ability of women to become greater activators of both their positive power and their wisdom.

Star Points

★ Power has been associated with men and discouraged for women.

★ Social stereotypes of women and men have made it more difficult for women to use their power.

★ Power needs to be redefined.

★ Power is not domination or control.

★ Comfort with power takes time and a new mindset.

★ Power is a separate concept from control.

★ Power is personal effectiveness.

★ Power is the mind's immune system for healthy living.

★ Positive power is power-with not power-over.

★ Power–with is inspirational to others.

★ Positive power utilizes the wisdom of women.

★ Positive power is the mind's glow.

★ Positive power allows women to create balance in their lives, fosters psychological well-being, and maintains physical health.

★ Positive power skills are the key to effective living in the new millennium and moving beyond the Glass Ceiling.

2

Power
Robbers

"Ordinary life widens the horizon for men.
Women are walled-in behind social convention."
—Dame Emilia Dilke, French Political Activist

The Experience

Have you ever felt robbed of power? Have you ever felt stymied? Have you ever felt overwhelmed and unable to achieve your objectives? Have you ever felt pulled in so many directions that you experience feelings of despair? Have you ever felt conflicted and torn between different options? Have you ever looked at your male colleagues and wondered how they were able to function with apparently less turmoil? Have you ever felt very frustrated and thwarted in achieving your goals? Have you ever just wanted to scream out your frustrations? If you have experienced any of the above, then you have experienced the impact of a power robber.

The women of the Women of Wisdom Power Breakfast Group are all successful achievers, yet, at times, each has experienced the loss of their power. I want to extend a special appreciation to the Women of Wisdom Power Breakfast Group for their continuing willingness to serve as examples to help others. Many of the members of the group chose to personally tell their stories without anonymity. The Women of Wisdom Power Breakfast Group was formed for women who had begun to experience the Glass Ceiling and who had been the mentors for many others. The theme for the group was "Who Mentors the Mentors?" The group's commitment to mentoring led some of the group members to decide to be personal examples for your benefit. As a psychologist, I am bound by the limits of confidentiality to protect the identity of the patients represented in the clinical cases presented in this book. The Women of Wisdom Power Breakfast Group, however, was not a therapy group. These women elected to be used as a focus group for this book, and shared the common theme of powerful women learning to be more effective in their usage of power. Although each individual member of the Women of Wisdom Power Breakfast Group is a leader in her own profession, each still struggles with the power robbers.

The power robbers are factors that will always impact your life. The crucial key to reducing power loss is to be aware of the power-robbing socialization messages that women receive and learn to counter these earlier messages with new lessons and new tools. The members of the Women of Wisdom Power Breakfast Group chose to reveal their power-robbing struggles, and in the revelation allowed themselves to be role models for each of you. Power robber messages are ongoing life variables that need to be monitored.

How Power Robbers Develop

Power robbers are the subtle socialization messages that women receive as they grow up. None of these subtle messages can be totally eliminated from your life. However, you will find as you review each of the top ten power robbers that each power robber also has affirmations to counter these thoughts. Using counter thoughts is a behavioral procedure which is part of a cognitive restructuring clinical intervention. Cognitive restructuring considers the framework—the outlook that we possess—impacts our behaviors and emotions. The psychological principal is: beliefs generate thoughts which generate emotions which impact our behaviors. A helpful image is to think of a cognitive framework as the frame of a picture. The frame of a picture is going to dramatically impact the visual appeal of that picture. Many times a different frame and matting will totally change the artistic appeal of the picture. In this same way, our ability to change our framework with different thoughts will generate different emotions and behaviors.

Internal messages are self-talk, which form our belief system, and are absorbed throughout our life journey. These messages are transmitted through family, friends, and peers. Often, the messages are not communicated directly through speech. The messages are frequently communicated by a subtle reward system. For example, you may never be directly told to be quiet and have a low profile in a group. However, every time you take the initiative and speak up at the dinner table, you are given disapproving looks by your parents and your brothers. Thus, the subtle message is to be quiet. On the other hand, every time your brother speaks up he is rewarded with encouragement and approving glances. It becomes very evident by the differential response to your behaviors that different expectations exist for women and men. These subtle socialization messages are power robbers for women.

The societal messages of different expectations for women and men combine to create stereotypic expectations by gender. The American Psychological Association published a recent report in *The APA Monitor* that discusses the impact of gender stereotypes. This report profiled the workplace in an article titled "Stereotypes Still Stymie Female Managers", and discussed multiple research studies which continue to report that female and male leaders received differential responses. This article and others clearly indicate that gender is an important factor in others' perceptions of appropriate behavior in life settings.

The APA article featured results of a study conducted by Catalyst, an organization studying women in the workplace. This study reported women executives believe that male stereotyping and preconceptions of women constitute fifty-two percent (52%) of the factors which create the Glass Ceiling. These opinions of the executive women contrast with the opinions of male Chief Executive Officers of corporations. The male executives view of why women are not penetrating the Glass Ceiling is attributed eight-two percent (82%) to be women's lack of general management and line experience and sixty-four percent (64%) because women have not been in the management pipeline long enough. Given the number of years that women have been in the workforce and the fact that they now comprise forty-six percent (46%) of that workforce, this viewpoint creates some question of male denial. A *Working Woman Magazine* surveyed corporate women of the breakthrough generation, and found seventy-eight percent (78%) of women indicated that the major hurdle for leadership positions was the tendency of male executives to select other males. Glass Ceiling researchers are advocating that promotion decision-making must be watched and records kept to equalize opportunities.

However, the denial of the amount of impact of socialization messages may be unintentional. Subtle messages that are carried in the culture often operate automatically with minimal awareness by the individual. Although Chief Executive Officers attribute the minimal presence of women in higher leadership positions to inexperience, they also do acknowledge that there is a twenty-five percent (25%) barrier to women advancing to leadership positions because of stereotyping and preconceptions of women. As the new millennium approaches, women need to actively and consciously change female stereotypes.

One of the most potent ways to alter stereotypes of women is to engage in positive power behaviors. Even in the 1990s, many women appear to suffer from power anorexia. If you think about your behaviors, think of the times that you do not engage in powerful behaviors. How many times does your cultural upbringing cause you to repress your viewpoints in order to accommodate and please others? A significant power robber for women is to seek acceptance rather than to be proactively empowered.

Joanne's Story

The subtle socialization and stereotypes of women cause many women to falter rather than move forward in powerful control of their world. Many executive women, despite considerable achievements, continue to wage war with the power robbers. As vice-president of her corporation, Joanne was referred for therapy for panic attacks. she was referred to my office by her cardiologist who had ruled out any heart difficulties. Joanne was in her early forties, and was a woman trapped into pleasing her mother, her three children, her business partner, and her husband. Pulled in a myriad of directions, her body was "short circuiting" and creating panic attacks. During cognitive-behavioral treatment, Joanne began to understand some of the internal self-talk that was requiring her always to be accommodating and engage in obsessive worrying behaviors. Joanne had difficulty in setting limits, tolerating conflicts, and negotiating her own needs. Joanne started each day with a "to do" list that exceded the number of hours in a day. Her unrealistic assumption of tasks was her undoing. Treatment included new power skills which allowed her to reduce the power robbers in her life. Joanne's utilization of positive power lessons and tools resulted in an elimination of her panic attacks in four months. Numerous clinical cases in her office have demonstrated that increasing awareness of power robbers combined with training in positive power tools can result in a decrease of emotional turmoil.

Acquiring Positive Power Skills

This chapter and the following chapter present a two-step process for acquiring positive power skills. The first step to behavior change is an awareness of nonproductive behaviors. This chapter discusses ten of the most significant power-robbing social messages for women. Identifying power robbers is critical, enabling women to shed their power anorexia and assume appropriate positive power. Once identified, the nonproductive power robber behaviors can be moderated and controlled.

As you grow up, many messages of how to behave are communicated. Messages of the past are never totally eliminated. Past messages need to be examined and adjusted as you increase in age and wisdom. Once again, I caution you against all-or-nothing thinking. Although it is tempting to categorize behaviors as those you want to retain and those you want to eliminate, in reality, most behaviors are on a continuum. As we examine each of the power robbers, we will find that, at times, some of the power-robbing behaviors are very appropriate. The power-robbing aspect of these behaviors needs to be continuously evaluated and adjusted for different life situations.

The purpose of identifying the top ten power robbers is to recognize potential roadblocks to effective functioning. As you develop your positive power tools, identifying those ten crucial, subtle socialization messages that are barriers to your power is the first step toward developing positive power tools. As I move forward to an in-depth discussion of the ten most significant power robbers, we also must face the sad reality that one of the unique issues for some women is their past life experiences of being victimized. When you suffer the psychological trauma of victimization, a sense of powerlessness invades your being. For victimized women, the positive power-training is even more crucial. Their past traumas have left them more vulnerable to the power robbers. However, victimization also can be used as a powerful life experience to increase your resiliency. While victimization is a life experience, it does not have to be an ongoing barrier in your life.

Wendy's Story

As you shall see later, the Second Wave of feminism in the latter half of the twentieth century made major contributions to increasing the awareness of abuse against women and "turning the tide" to women's rights and protection for women. With this greater awareness came greater freedom to seek help to overcome victimization. A significant number of patients have demonstrated with their life changes that the impact of victimization can be altered. For example, Wendy was physically abused by her father and had turned to drugs and food. When she first entered therapy, she was addicted to crack, overusing alcohol and other drugs, and was extremely obese. Her life had gone steadily downhill, and she lost her job and was thrown out of one drug rehabilitation program after another. Wendy made multiple attempts on her life, often slashing her wrists and arms and self-mutilating her body. During initial sessions, Wendy stated "I'm a loser . . . Why should I bother? . . . Feeling the pain of cutting is what I deserve." Today, Wendy is a testimony to the changes that women can make once they begin to shed their powerlessness and develop new positive power skills.

Wendy, although she is still in treatment, has been off of drugs for three years, is training for a new career, and has lost over fifty pounds. Both physically and psychologically, Wendy is a dramatically changed woman. she has the ability to live independently, make productive life choices, and continues to establish new goals. In a recent session, Wendy stated, "I never believed I would be alive now . . . I never thought reacting differently would make such a difference."

In many ways, my view of therapy for victimized women is power-training for productive living. For all women, life-coaching is necessary to offset the subtle power-robbing messages of women's socialization patterns. The theme of training women in positive power skills for productive living has been consistent in my work with the formation of the Women of Wisdom Power Breakfast Group, the presentations at regional and national meetings, and the life-coaching conducted in my private practice. I have seen that acquiring skills and fine-tuning these skills is a lifelong process. You will now embark on an awareness and elimination of the power robbers.

Female Stereotypes

Women are strongly encouraged to be sweet, calm, gentle, and always helpful to others. You are encouraged to be a people-pleaser who will generate positive feelings in others. Being liked and accepted becomes a strong impetus for all women. In many ways you are running for the "Miss Congeniality" award in your circle of family, friends, and colleagues. This behavior of accommodating and pleasing, however, causes many women to give away their personal power. Pat Schroeder, the former Colorado Congresswoman and President of the Association of American Publishers, stated that "Many women have more power than they recognize, and they're very hesitant to use it, for they fear they won't be loved."

Certainly, I am not suggesting that one should be adversarial or nasty. Many instances exist where you want and will try to be accommodating and pleasing to others. Constant accommodation, however, does not allow you to negotiate your own needs. Moreover, constant people-pleasing shifts your focus to concentrating on others versus awareness and consideration of your own needs. The "other-focus", as a primary focus, is a frequent and significant problem for women. Women need to take into account their own needs, desires, and goals.

The difficulties that women have in identifying and focusing on their own needs, wants, and goals may be reflective of the biological template that each woman possesses. As a woman, you have a biological template to reproduce. A portion of this template requires a genetic programming for nurturing. In the early days of civilization, the cave woman needed a genetic programming to allow her to breast-feed and protect her offspring. This biological template is part of your genetic programming today. This nurturing template plays a significant role in the development of people-pleasing behaviors. The interaction of this genetic template with societal messages generates people-pleasing behaviors, which can be carried to the extreme.

The people-pleasing behaviors of women are a significant variable as to why women have twice the depression rate versus men. This gender frequency for depression is an international statistic that crosses cultural boundaries. People-pleasing behaviors cause a focus on accommodation that often places women in an overwhelmed position with few of their own wants, needs, or goals being met. This imbalance inevitably leads to anger and frustration that is difficult to solve. Many times depression is viewed as anger turned inward.

Being a people-pleaser and accommodating others results in you meeting little of your own needs. If needing to accommodate and please others is paramount, then you do not have the ability to refuse requests that may not be in your best interest. Each time you lose the ability to refuse a request, you give away some of your personal power. Additionally, the fear of not pleasing others is that disapproval will result. For many women, disapproval is very painful. The fear of disapproval and its pain may cause you to look for affirmation from others. Thus, you might ask someone: "Don't you agree?" or "Would you say this is an appropriate point?" This searching for affirmation and confirmation creates a danger that you may be viewed as an indecisive individual. Indecisive individuals are not promoted to upper level management positions.

As an accommodating people-pleaser, you expect that your caretaking efforts will be rewarded. Unfortunately this is not always the case. People with whom you interact may or may not give you reciprocal consideration. Treating others in a pleasing manner at times is appropriate. However, there is no requirement that people will act kindly toward you. Thus, one of the dangers of people-pleasing is that when people are unpleasant in return, you take it personally. If you are less invested in people-pleasing behaviors, you are less vulnerable to interpreting others behaviors toward you in a personal manner.

In summary, the power-robbing characteristics of being an accommodating people-pleaser fall into three categories. The first category is that you place yourself in danger of not meeting your own wants, needs, and goals. The second category is that you may present yourself as indecisive in your search for affirmation and checking-in with others. The third characteristic is that you respond in a very personal manner to all interactions where you are invested in receiving positive feedback from others.

A consistent pattern of accommodating, people-pleasing behaviors creates vulnerabilities on multiple fronts. Thoughtful and considerate behaviors to others need to be distinguished from the nonproductive, over-accommodating, people-pleasing behavior pattern. The "over-doers" put the rights and needs of others first. The thoughtful and considerate individual respects the rights and needs of others and places their own rights and needs in the equation.

Research consistently confirms the existence of broad social-cultural attitudes that limit women's possibilities and undermine their ability to activate their power. Patriarchy and sexism have been responsible for a differential socialization of the sexes and the prevalence of gender related evaluations. Patriarchal socialization positively reinforces the accepted male behaviors, allowing men to expand on their experiences. In the same way, the androcentrism of society has used male behaviors as the "ideal" or "benchmark" of how to act, and this measuring stick subjugates woman to "the other" and inferior role, shaped and confined by a prejudicial benchmark. The daily life stressors that characterize the lives of many women are linked to the limitations of these societal roles.

The reality is that ordinary life tends to widen the horizons of opportunities for men, while narrowing opportunities for women, who often find themselves boxed in by subtle social messages and constraints. Sandy Bem described this narrowing and widening focus in her Gender Schema Theory, where she noted gender lenses that become imbedded in our culture and create variable social practices that are taught to children in many subtle ways. For women, "gender lenses" at times can be a detrimental barrier.

The ten power robbers will be set out, along with the messages society gives us—messages that reinforce these power robbers and give them continuing strength. To determine whether you may be personally affected by a particular power robber, review the questions given with each power robber. If you answer any of these with a "yes," then you may need to work on that particular power robber using the counter thoughts which are presented at the end of each section. To determine the impact that certain power robbers may have. I have also included a short psychological test and scoring of your answers at the end of the chapter.

POWER ROBBER #1

**If I am accommodating and pleasing, I will
have many friends and a rewarding life.**

Messages from Society

➤ Can you remember being told to be a good girl and a nice girl?

➤ All good things come to good girls and nice girls.

➤ Be agreeable and everyone will like you.

➤ You need to have friends.

➤ How popular you are is very important.

Questions to Ask Yourself

___ Are you very concerned that the majority of other people like you?

___ Are you always concerned about others' opinions?

___ Is it very important to you that you not disappoint others?

___ Do you have difficulty saying no?

___ Do you feel guilty when you disappoint someone?

Breakfast Club Story

Terry Santini is a successful CPA, the owner of her own firm and was an elected official the former Vice Mayor of Davie, Florida. Terry's grandparents were born in Lebanon and immigrated to the United States. The Lebanese culture teaches women to be submissive and the primary role of women is to bear children and to serve their family. Terry was raised in South Boston, Massachusetts, with other Middle Eastern immigrant families that carried on the traditions of the old country. During her childhood, she remembers her father calling across the house so that she could change the television station or fetch him an ashtray.

Terry grew up with three brothers, and the message that she received was that the family business would have openings for her brothers and for any husband that she married, but not for her. Throughout her life, Terry strove to accommodate and please others. A personal crisis in 1991 mobilized Terry to break out of her over-accommodating, people-pleasing pattern. Her youngest son was five-and-a-half years old and had been hospitalized with a serious illness for eleven days. The pediatrician could not find anything wrong with her son and was planning to send him home with parasite medication. Fearing for her son's life caused Terry, on her own instincts, to powerfully insist that additional testing be conducted. As a result of the testing, her son was diagnosed with Burkitt's Lymphoma, the fastest growing cancer known, doubling in size every twenty-four hours. A tumor was located in her son's intestine and would have burst within a few days. Her son received surgery, and very aggressive chemotherapy was recommended. Terry's husband was am-bivalent about the aggressive chemotherapy drugs, and the next day Terry found herself, once again, in an unusual position. She became the primary decision-maker to move forward with the chemotherapy. Her son responded to the treatment and remains in remission today.

For Terry, shedding her former people-pleasing behavior with both the physician and her spouse was the beginning of a major life transition. Terry no longer places the approval of others as her highest priority. Although she is a considerate and thoughtful woman, she establishes her own goals, mobilizes to have her own needs met, and moderates her people-pleasing urges.

Overview

The recognition that women need to shed their pleasing behav-iors has been encouraged in numerous texts. A recent book, *Goodbye Good Girl,* stated that "Constantly trying to conform to expectations eventually saps all of your energy until you are limp as a doormat and not exactly in the position to exert a positive influence on the world." Often a book title gives us insight to messages that need to be heard. *Goodbye Good Girl* is a title that reflects the need to shed behaviors of over-accommodation and people-pleasing. It is interesting to note that two recent books, *Bad Girls Good Girls: Women, Sex, and Power in the Nineties* and *Goodbye Good Girl,* encourage women to let go of the "rules" and recognize problematic patterns in the socialization of women.

Endless pleasing of others robs you of your power. Unfortunately, the difficulty in managing this behavior is the frequent societal rewarding of the behaviors—women are always praised for pleasing others. You also get reinforcement from others by not disappointing them. However, a source of power lies in the ability to give yourself the same kind of care that you would give to others.

People-pleasing thinking often leads to indecisiveness by relying upon the opinions of others to determine your actions. The cornerstone of this behavior is the belief that if you can get others to be pleased with you and approve of you, then you will feel better inside. Actually, the opposite happens when you try to please everybody. It is an impossible task and wears thin very quickly. You begin to lose your own self-respect and become resentful of the people you are trying to please. You do not want to be viewed merely as a hard-working-worker-bee, a rubberstamp worker without the ability to achieve higher positions. Sometimes you need to make tough decisions that will not please people, that can, indeed, upset people. Your growth and opportunities will be limited, without a willingness to make hard-line decisions.

Counter Thoughts

1. Someone being disappointed in me is not a life or death matter.
2. Feelings are not a virus in the air—I am responsible for my own feelings and choose my own feelings.
3. My happiness comes from within, not from without. I do not depend on approval from the outside world to make me happy.
4. I am committed to a program of self-approval and self-affirmation on a daily basis.
5. Others' opinions do not equal me. If someone does not like me or rejects me, this does not diminish me in any way, this is only their opinion.
6. Being liked and approved by others is favorable, but not necessary.
7. I can make choices that nurture me.
8. I want to share my life *with* others, not sacrifice my life *for* others.

POWER ROBBER #2

I want to do it right and not make mistakes.

Messages from Society

➢ It is more important to get it right rather than finish it.

➢ You don't want to be embarrassed by making a mistake.

➢ Mistakes are to be avoided at all costs; take all the time you need to do it right.

Do you remember being told to be careful? Make sure you do it right! Don't make any mistakes now! That is the beginning of the power-robbing message of perfection, the installation of the fear of making mistakes. The desire to always do it right and not make mistakes often leads to the trap of perfectionism. Perfectionist individuals are extremely critical, and have a high level of dissatisfaction. Your drive for perfection causes you to set up unrealistic expectations, which can lead to a failure cycle. In life, perfection does not exist. You need to readjust your thinking to the concept of adequate behaviors.

Questions to Ask Yourself

___ Do you believe that all your work must be done preferably better than other people do it?

___ Do you go to any lengths to avoid mistakes?

___ Do you scold and criticize yourself when you make mistakes?

___ Do you feel you have to work twice as hard as "truly successful people" in order to succeed?

___ Do you believe that one mistake ruins everything?

___ Do you agonize over mistakes that you make and try to make amends for what you have done?

Breakfast Club Story

Amy Arnold was the oldest of two children, raised in Akron, Ohio. In the eighth grade, Amy decided that she wanted to be a veterinarian. However, she was allergic to animals and it soon became clear that this would be an unrealistic career goal. Her mother instead encouraged her to be a "people doctor." From early childhood, Amy was encouraged to do anything that she desired. However, she was also expected to be exceptional. Outstanding accomplishments were barely recognized and seldom rewarded. Amy adopted these, sometimes unrealistic, expectations as her own, and became a hard-driving overachiever. As she moved forward in her college career, she found herself drawn to plastic surgery, and after her training as a general surgeon, she continued in her studies as a plastic surgeon.

Amy feels a strong need to "be the best." If she found herself not being the best, she often would withdraw from the situation and would not continue. During her senior residency, Amy had a life-changing experience. She discovered that she had made a charting error on a pediatric surgical floor. The charting error was quickly noticed, and there were no negative results to the patient. However, Amy's perfectionist style and highly critical behaviors caused her to be devastated by her mistake.

At that time, Amy actually thought of quitting medicine. It was her male chairman who was able to counsel Amy. He coached her to understand human beings cannot be robots and some mistakes are inevitable. Fortunately, the perceptive interventions of her chairman caused her to step back and reassess. For the first time, Amy challenged her perfectionist belief system, and began a journey of self-acceptance of human mistakes and an adjustment of her expectations. Amy completed her training and is recognized as an outstanding plastic surgeon. However, even today, Amy has to actively monitor her behaviors to maintain realistic expectations and to avoid being highly critical of herself.

Overview

Avoidance of mistakes is unrealistic. Mistakes are part and parcel of a learning process. Mistake avoidance is a drive for perfection. Often a deep-seated fear of failure and rejection is underneath the drive for perfection. This fear causes you to be your own critic. When failure ultimately occurs due to unrealistic expectations, perfectionists rebuke themselves and withdraw. This fear of failure can be a businessperson's biggest stumbling block. Being fearful leads to staying with safe behaviors and not "push the envelope." Leadership requires moving beyond safe behaviors with creative initiative. You need to "push the envelope" to create a higher probability of having success. If you are always staying in a safe zone to avoid mistakes, your success will be limited. You need to put out effort with a willingness to absorb mistakes. A hidden danger of perfectionism and a fearfulness of mistakes is that you become so focused on "doing it right" that you often do not have your antenna out for the political atmosphere. In the majority of cases, multiple right ways of doing something exist. You can go down multiple paths to reach the same outcome. A fearfulness of mistakes can cause a rigidity which limits an openness to achieving business goals in another manner. As part of a management team, a woman's openness to other options is crucial.

Perfectionism can be a trap that saps our energy and bogs down our career path. Although, of course, work must be well done, each work sample does not have to be a work of art. Performance standards must be viewed from a cost-benefit analysis of value received for the effort taken. All tasks can be redone ad nauseum, and at some point "enough is enough."

Quality work can be completed in time efficient means. Productivity and an ability to move to the next task are essential. A large element of perfectionism is avoiding criticism. However, if you avoid all criticism, you become paralyzed.

Mistakes will be integral to efficiently moving forward. People make mistakes from the beginning of their life to the end—whether it be the imperfect faltering movements of a toddler as she tries new steps, or some oversight as a manager—for mistakes will always happen. You want to tolerate criticism, tolerate errors, be open to different approaches, and move forward. Forward movement to your goals supercedes a concern with mistakes. Criticism avoiders find themselves focused on anticipating the reactions of others versus efficient work production and meeting their goals. No matter how excellent your work product, you cannot protect yourself from all criticism. Criticism is not career-stopping, but not meeting your goals may be a major issue limiting your opportunities. Thus, you need to tolerate mistakes, rebound from criticism, and maintain your momentum toward your goals.

Counter Thoughts

1. Perfection is an unrealistic expectation.
2. Seeking perfection is paralyzing.
3. I need to be my cheerleader, not my self-critic.
4. I want to be conscientious, not perfect.
5. I can only make the best decision at the time.
6. I want to strive for excellence, not perfection.
7. I can be myself; I do not have to prove myself.
8. I see my mistakes only as temporary setbacks and learning opportunities.

POWER ROBBER #3

I obtain security in life by finding a suitable life partner.

Messages from Society

➤ You don't want to be alone in life.

➤ It is important that you find the right match and have someone to share your life.

➤ Life is very difficult if you are alone.

➤ You need to be protected.

Questions to Ask Yourself

—— Are you focused on being in a relationship?

—— Without a relationship, do you feel lost and frightened?

—— Do you have a low tolerance to being alone and enjoying your own company?

—— Is being totally responsible for yourself emotionally and financially frightening to you?

—— Do you feel you are adequately developing your own talents?

Francesca's Story

Francesca was born in an Italian family and from early days remembered receiving bride dolls for Christmas and being coached on "marrying the right man" and not on developing her own talents. A big excitement in the family was when she was invited to the Junior Prom as a freshman in high school. Her family was relieved to have her "man-search" begin, and her social life launched. Everyone was taking pictures as her Mother put on her rhinestone tiara. Her dress was strapless, although she had little to hold it up, with layers of ruffles. Does the image of a trussed-up turkey come to mind?

She remembered being in her sophomore year at college and becoming anxious that she did not have a steady boyfriend. she had been given a clear message that not only did she have to receive her bachelor's degree at school, she also needed to receive her "MRS. Degree." She found herself experiencing a great deal of pressure to locate a suitable mate. Her Italian family wanted her to have children while she was young to ensure healthy offspring. As a result, she joined a sorority and was conducting her search for a suitable husband. The sororities and fraternities had a "sister sorority brother fraternity" arrangement. she found her husband-to-be in the "brother fraternity."

Believing that her security was intricately linked to his career, she worked full-time, while her husband attended law school. She remembered being at one social event at the law school, where one of the professors asked me why she was not attending law school as well. She recalled being surprised at the question, as well as being puzzled. Her grades were strong and she had received more collegiate awards than her spouse. Yet, she had fallen into the trap of supporting the career goals of another as the key to her security.

Subsequently, like so many other women of her generation, she found herself divorced. It was only after the divorce that she began to increase her focus on developing her own skills, and to accept as a reality that her goal was to be economically self-sufficient. She recounted the excitement of buying her first property, and being able to decorate it totally to her own taste without having to consult anyone. The freedom of self-sufficiency was heady and exhilarating. She shifted her focus from an external search for security through others to the internal development of her own competencies. This shift led her, at the age of thirty-five, to return to school and obtain her medical degree.

One of the most significant barriers to women's utilization of power is the focus on security through others. Throughout your life, subtle cultural messages convey that security requires dependency on others. The "other-reliance" cognitive messages result in women being externally rather than internally grounded and neglecting their own self-growth opportunities to develop their own competencies.

Overview

The focus on security through others causes you to avoid new opportunities and avoid new experiences. A security focus causes you to want to stay with people that you know and know you, rather than electing to try new experiences. Just as a confining "safe zone" was created with avoiding mistakes, so is another growth stifling "safe zone" created when security is obtained only through others. Staying in known circles prevents you from creating new alliances and experiencing opportunities for growth wherever you may go.

This external seeking of security causes you to cling to the familiar emotional comfort of others that accept you and your values. You spend a lot of effort in doing what you are told, and expect to get security in return. Looking to others to protect you, sends you on a rollercoaster ride with a life determined by others.

The Noah's Ark image of two-by-two is engrained in our society. The difficulty arises when we perceive being a couple is essential to life functioning. This perception promotes a view of yourself as needy and somewhat helpless. Once security becomes external and requires caretaking by another, you loose your ability to control your own life. Relationships can be life-enhancing. However, it is important to see a relationship as *adding* to your life, rather than being *essential* to your life. An image that is helpful is seeing yourself as the cake. Relationships are the icing that can sweeten life. You provide the substance.

Counter Thoughts

1. I enjoy my relationships, but they are not my total life.
2. I have the ability to seek new relationships.
3. I have the ability to be employable and support myself.
4. I dedicate myself to the full development of my talents.
5. Aloneness is preferable to being trapped in a meaningless relationship.
6. The quality of my relationships is more important than being in a relationship at any cost.

Power Robber #4

I want to avoid upsetting others.

Messages from Society

➤ It is important to be a nice girl and not upset anybody.

➤ Remember good girls are always pleasant.

➤ Put your best face forward, don't let anyone know you are upset.

➤ If you can't say anything nice, keep quiet.

➤ You get more with honey than vinegar.

Questions to Ask Yourself

—— Do you find yourself apologizing prior to making a request?

—— Do you find yourself worrying about others' possible negative reactions?

—— When conflict begins to arise, do you find yourself engaging in soothing behaviors?

—— Do you blame yourself if a conflict does arise?

—— Are you unable to communicate your own frustrations or upset feelings directly?

Breakfast Club Story

Linda Grabowski's career in printing and graphic design began at her husband's urging. Shortly before her second child was born, her husband, David, had purchased a printing business with a co-worker from the hotel where he worked. As the first year of business proceeded, the partner elected to not continue with the printing business. David arrived home just before their second child's first birthday party with a set of keys to the business and an encouraging smile. The printing business had become her task.

Linda struggled significantly during her early years of managing the company. Her prior business experiences had been as a teacher for eight years, and as a mother. Linda soon found herself being the nurturer to her employees, being flexible and tolerant, and not wanting to upset any of her workers. These behaviors led to one of her employees getting out of control and refusing to take directions from her. In an example Linda related, she gave the employee a clear directive, and he refused to comply, then proceeded to throw the cash drawer in the air. Linda's exceptional tolerance as a manager had led to her own personal abuse.

Slowly, Linda began to maintain her tolerance and nurturing, but coupled these behaviors with the development of limits. Linda began to recognize that she was not helping herself or her employees by not setting acceptable standards of performance. Being a supportive manager did not mean being a manager who tolerates any and all behaviors from employees. Every business, to be cost-effective, must have standards and maintain a level of productivity. As Linda began to place in perspective the feelings of others and balance this perspective with productivity, her business stress became reduced and the business increased. Linda now recognizes that some conflict is inevitable in management.

Overview

The underlying premise of the message to not upset others is based on an irrational belief. The irrational belief is that you can control someone else's feelings with your behaviors. We do not have the power to creates feelings in others, or dictate feelings to others. Each individual is responsible for her own beliefs and thought patterns which in turn creates her own feelings. Thus, it is impossible to be able to predict what behaviors will upset others. You can be acting in a charming manner and still receive an upset response.

Not only are you unable to control another's reaction to you, but life necessitates a degree of conflict. Going out of your way to avoid conflict also avoids constructive confrontation, prevents decision-making, and creates a wishy-washy persona. If you always attempt to avoid upsetting others, you become a social chameleon. Conflict is an inevitable part of life and you need to develop appropriate conflict resolution skills. Avoiding conflict robs you of the ability to develop these skills. The danger of being a social chameleon is that you are so agreeable that you become a "yes person." As a "yes person" you reduce some of your authority and credibility, and decrease the possibility you will move beyond the Glass Ceiling.

Women have long received a strong societal message to not "ruffle any feathers." Women are continually cast into the role of peacemaker. Not only is the avoidance of upsetting others and conflict unrealistic, but such avoidance also predisposes women to constant apologizing to avoid any negative feelings. The pattern of always saying, "I'm sorry," creates an image of powerlessness and engenders condescending behaviors. These images and reactions do not help women position themselves as potential leaders.

The flip side of not upsetting anyone means that you cannot express any feelings of being upset yourself or discuss any angry feelings. Women are coached not to express negative feelings because it will damage relationships. Women are always encouraged to remain calm. This suppression of anger produces high frustration, feelings of weakness, lowers self-esteem, and limits your effectiveness. When you hold back your reactions, you are not interacting with others realistically. You are placing yourself in danger of being mistreated because you are not alerting others to their problem behaviors. You need to respect yourself and request respect from others to be effective, productive, and recognized for your leadership skills.

Counter Thoughts

1. I am not responsible for the feelings of others.
2. Someone liking me is not a life or death matter.
3. There is more than one way of looking at things and I am entitled to my opinion.

4. I have the right to express annoyances and do not have to escalate into anger.
5. I recognize that conflict is an inevitable part of life.
6. I can engage in constructive conflict and not damage my relationships.
7. I need to give feedback on problem behaviors so adjustments can be made.
8. I want to be considerate and effective.

POWER ROBBER #5

I need to be polite and not make direct requests.

Messages from Society

➤ Remember it is very rude to ask for anything.

➤ Wait for people to ask you; it is rude to make requests.

➤ Be a polite, nice girl and don't make demands.

➤ Be quiet and sweet and you will be rewarded.

Questions to Ask Yourself

— Do you proceed your requests with a permission-giving phrase such as, may I, can I, do you think?

— Are you overusing the "I" pronoun in your request statements?

— Do you approach a request in a deferential manner?

— Do you ask for permission before you ask a question?

— Do you take the time to organize your requests?

— Do you avoid making requests?

Helen's Story

Helen was reared by parents who were doctoral level research scientists. Both were polite and non-confrontational in the family setting. Throughout her early years, Helen was constantly encouraged to wait her turn like a lady, and always to be lady-like. Helen was an only child and her parents encouraged adult, in-control behaviors. She was expected to be obedient and make minimal requests.

Although Helen has impeccable manners, her early emphasis on politeness and directness caused her difficulties. Helen experienced an early success manufacturing baby clothes. However, her inability to ask direct questions caused her to have difficulty in negotiations, and eventually the company went out of business. Helen had been unable to capitalize on buyout offers. The "lady" was unable to negotiate an effective arrangement. Politeness became a business barrier. She could produce an excellent product, manage her employees, but could not grow her business through vendor negotiations or offers from potential investors.

After this draining business experience, Helen recognized that it was important for her to avoid business ownership. Although she had creative ideas, her years of polite, accommodating behaviors hampered her ability to conduct business. She returned to college and became a professor in women's studies. The academic environment maintained her comfort zone. Moreover, Helen mentors her students to learn power skills, which will maximize their abilities to be successful in the business world.

Overview

Courtesy to others is an appropriate sign of mutual respect. However, overly deferential politeness and indirectness undermines your ability to reach your goals. Being overly polite and indirect creates an image of passivity and a lack of strength. Examples of indirectness are: I just wanted, I wondered if, may I ask a question, and I only wanted to know about it. Direct requests are how, what, when, where, why, and who. Direct requests improve the clarity of communication.

Women are subtly socialized to be indirect and also to overdo the utilization of the pronoun "I". "I" statements can be very helpful in situations where you want to avoid being accusatory with the "you" statement. However, "I" statements work best if you are referring to yourself directly. Women need to learn to engage in more powerful dialogues. For example, "I don't have enough time to finish the project" would be better translated to "The tentative schedule does not allow for completion of the project" or "Let's have a meeting and reassess the priority schedule for the project." The focus away from personalization pronoun "I" is a more direct communication pattern and controls the female tendency for indirectness. In these examples, the direct communication pattern also keeps the focus on the schedule, and not on personal performance.

Women are encouraged to be deferential which creates a behavior pattern of asking permission, waiting for the right moment to initiate a request, and waiting for opportunities, rather than creating opportunities. By waiting for others to take the initiative, you avoid the risk of any rejection or disagreement. However, you also limit your opportunities. You become constricted and limit your communication effectiveness. You hold back and waste time.

As evidenced in the socialization pattern of other power robbers, a consistent theme exists for women to stay "safe" and not do anything that would be misconstrued or offensive to anyone. This places women in a double bind of preventing them from creating a direct path to their goal. Not only are your goals made more difficult to reach, you engage in "double-speak" versus clarity. Examples of this problematic "double-speak" and the hidden message of asking permission are the following:

Example 1: Indirect request: "Could you please double-check your email, I did not get a reply from the email that I sent you last week?"

Direct request: "Here is a hardcopy of the high priority email. Let's take a few minutes to review it together; a decision has to be made."

Example 2: Indirect request: "I found a very interesting convention that might be helpful in planning for my new management team. Would you mind, within the next week, sitting down and evaluating it with me?"

Direct request: "Here is a superb conference that dovetails exactly with the new management project that you assigned me. I recommend that this immediately be included in my convention plans for the year."

The ability to make direct requests is essential to goal achievement. These requests must be stated in the most powerful manner which avoids any image of asking permission. Women, with their programming for indirectness, have a tendency to talk around the issues rather than to get to the bottom line. The more directness you possess, the more clarity you will have in your communications. You will increase the probability of receiving your requests and be able to reach your goals with more ease.

Counter Thoughts

1. I can be courteous without being deferentially polite.
2. Making requests does not require asking permission.
3. I have the right to ask directly.
4. Indirectness slows the progress toward my goals.
5. Efficiency requires initiative.
6. Direct requests are necessary for effective communication.
7. Clarity in communication brings you closer to your goals.

POWER ROBBER #6

I need to treat everyone equally.

Messages from Society

➤ Watch out—be sure to be fair.

➤ You need to treat everyone equally.

➤ You wouldn't want to be left out—be sure you include everyone.

➤ Don't show favoritism.

Questions to Ask Yourself

— Do you find yourself carefully evaluating how much time you spend with each of your friends?

— Do you find yourself worrying about whether you are spending as much money on a gift for one person as you did for another?

— Do you find yourself being concerned that someone might suspect you of favoritism?

— Do you find yourself being concerned that someone might think you are an "apple polisher" who is paying too much attention to upper management?

— Do you find yourself worrying about being fair in the office?

— Do you often say life is not fair?

Breakfast Club Story

Heidi Richards has been in the florist business for seventeen years. Prior to that time, she was an entrepreneur in a daycare center. Heidi, who is an author herself, has been an involved community leader, founder of the Women's Chamber of Commerce of Broward County as well as a leader in her industry. As the concepts of the power robbers were discussed, Heidi acknowledged that "I want to be viewed as fair and just; I am very concerned with others' judgment of me." As the discussion continued, Heidi indicated her conflicted emotions with the realities of being a business owner. She stated, "If a major customer, who is contributing twenty to thirty thousand dollars to my bottom line, calls at 4:00 P.M., that customer will have the flowers delivered by me personally if necessary. Although I strive to give superior service to all of my customers, clearly, business realities have to be addressed. I could not provide that service to everyone."

Heidi also discussed the difficulties of balancing fairness with the conflicting demands of employees. Inevitably, one of her employees will ask for special favors. While in most companies, seniority is perceived as a significant positive factor in making requests, Heidi struggles with keeping the perspective of the impact on other employees. Her constant concern with fairness and equal treatment generates additional business pressures. Heidi personifies the struggles of a businesswoman, who on one hand can make the necessary business decisions and, on the other hand, struggles to do so without guilt.

Overview

Women appear to be imbued with an idealistic view that if you treat others fairly, people will treat you fairly. In addition to believing in the "reciprocal fairness" theory, women also believe that fairness is essential. However, in many ways, fairness is a subjective perception. The reality of life is sometimes different. You want to be supportive of others, but you need to consider carefully the dangers of not individualizing your interactions with others. If you possess the idea of fair and equal treatment to everyone—independent of their work productivity, independent of what a customer may add to the bottom line, independent of the reciprocal benefits—it will be difficult for you to take on the role of a leader or be adequately effective in your life.

Many business and personal situations exist where differential treatment has to be considered. The fairness theory leaves you vulnerable to power drains of energy. If you continue to accommodate everyone equally, you are not preserving your energy. You need to consider the reciprocity of your relationships, and invest your energies in relationships where reciprocity and benefits exist.

The concept of "equality for fairness" also presents problems in terms of time. If you treat everyone equally, you are going to give away the precious commodity of time because you are going to speak to everyone equally. Particularly in terms of time management, you will find it is essential to make assessments to maintain your own productivity and control over your time.

While we certainly need to recognize that consideration of others is essential, fairness and equal treatment should be only *part* of the variables in your decision-making equation. Adequate decision-making must include an assessment of time variables, productivity variables, financial variables, reciprocity variables, and benefit variables. People with effective power consider all the variables and make decisions accordingly. Women need to recognize we have to fairly assess *all* variables, and then move forward.

Counter Thoughts

1. Different people add differently to my life.
2. I need to realize that differential treatment is not unfair treatment.
3. Different circumstances need to be responded to with different behaviors.
4. Life is not a neat process where everything can be given out in equal measure.
5. Each situation must be evaluated independently with consideration of many variables.

POWER ROBBER #7

I need to obey the rules.

Messages from Society

➤ Good girls obey at all times.

➤ If you are a lady, you will follow the rules.

➤ Acting proper is important.

➤ Girls don't make a mess.

➤ Following the rules leads to success.

Questions to Ask Yourself

— Do you always follow the rules?

— Do you ever question the sensibility of rules?

— Do you never allow yourself to make an exception to the rules?

— Is being viewed as obedient important to you?

— When deviating from the rules, do you feel guilty?

Breakfast Club Story

Carol Rudd is a religious woman who was brought up strictly, and told on numerous occasions that she must "do the right thing." A difficult time in her life ensued when her husband was admitted to the hospital for an operation. Unfortunately, her husband, who was a young sixty-four, died as a result of the operation. Carol had some very serious misgivings on the quality of medical care that her husband received. However, due to her strict adherence to following the rules and listening to authority, she found it very difficult to pursue alternative medical resources. She acted appropriately in line with her upbringing and followed the strict rules of allowing the physician to manage her husband's case.

Carol continues to struggle between her following the rules belief, and her strong intuitive feeling that her husband may have died unnecessarily. When you obey the rules with a blind acceptance, you are placing yourself at a large risk for significant turmoil. Carol's rule-following dictum compounded the tragedy of her spouse's death. She daily chastises herself for her inability to be an active member of her husband's medical team. Would her husband have died if she had been able to take more initiative? Is she experiencing survivor guilt? Was the medical care adequate and her husband's death unavoidable?

No answers are available to these questions. As Carol chose this power robber, she clearly communicates that her dutiful, rule-following beliefs sabotaged her abilities in a time of crisis. Rules can be arbitrary. At times, rules need to be broken.

Overview

The gender rules on obedience are flagrantly different. The tolerance for boys to be naughty and mischievous is dramatically high. The expectation that boys need to act out, after all this is just "boys being boys," is prevalent in society. Boys naturally disobey occasionally to "test their limits." However, minimal tolerance exists for acting-out behaviors for girls. Girls are expected to walk a narrow line. If a girl is not acting in a prim, proper, and ladylike manner, she is immediately termed a tomboy and looked at askance. Even in the classroom, teachers tolerate boys yelling out the answers. However, it is important that the girls raise their hands, then wait to be acknowledged.

This "good girl programming" to be obedient and to wait to be acknowledged will result in you waiting your whole life. The rules can be different for different people. So although you want to be respectful of the rules, a blind following of the rules is foolhardy and problematic.

A blind obedience to the rules creates a naiveté and makes it difficult for women to engage in meaningful negotiations. Rule-following may cause a woman to assume that the only response to a first request is to automatically meet the request, rather than negotiating with a counter proposal. A strong adherence to rules limits opportunity, making flexible and creative responses difficult. Remember, outrageous, rule-breaking decisions may lead to phenomenal success!

Counter Thoughts

1. Rules cannot cover all circumstances.
2. Rules need to be bent to fit the situation.
3. Rules are general guidelines—not laws.
4. Rules can be creatively applied.
5. For every rule, there is an exception.

POWER ROBBER #8

If there is a problem, it is my fault.

Messages from Society

➢ Remember you are the one that is responsible.

➢ You are the caretaker for others.

➢ Being responsible is very important.

➢ You need to watch out for others.

Questions to Ask Yourself

—— Do you find yourself asking: Oh my goodness, what did I do?

—— Do you question yourself regularly?

—— Do you spend a lot of time engaging in worry activities?

—— Do problems make you uncomfortable?

Breakfast Club Story

Andrea Lettman is an intelligent and experienced administrator. As an administrator in the healthcare industry, she deals with numerous administrative changes. Andrea had capably executed her administrative duties and corporate headquarters elected to give her a sizable bonus. When the bonus was entered into the payroll system, there was a significant reaction among the medical staff. Andrea was approached and told that she should have dispersed some of the money to the employees. Andrea's first reaction was to feel badly, to engage in self-blame and to feel like she had made an error.

She felt greedy, uncomfortable, and responsible for the differential bonus. Of course, she was responsible for her superior work, not the corporate bonus decision. Upset, worried, and contrite, Andrea went home and discussed the bonus crisis with her support network. Andrea's support network includes women and men. The women agonized with her. The men were incredulous: "How come you are not thrilled? This is a case of sour grapes. This is the reality of the evolution of medical practices to corporate business practices. Dismiss the feedback, and relish the fruits of your labor." Andrea had to be reminded of the business practices of corporations. In the corporate culture, administrative bonuses are specific to the individual and appropriate.

Once Andrea was able to look at the issue from a broader perspective, she was able to change her self-talk and enjoy her bonus. However, her initial instinct to immediately assume blame and feel guilty is a common reaction and a strong influence in many women's lives.

Overview

Women are conditioned to accept responsibility for everything. There are several jokes about problems in life being due to ineffective mothering. Mother and mother-in-law jokes proliferate. Women, with their biological template of nurturing, are vulnerable to being over-responsible. This over-responsibility causes them to assume blame for situations over which, in reality, they have no control.

Women's predisposition to worry and guilt feelings cause them to blame themselves for problems. When problems arise, women become uncomfortable and engage in immediate worry that in some way they may have caused the problem. Worry can be a destructive emotion, and guilty feelings compound worry. Even physical impairment can result from excessive concerns and guilt. Worry is often referred to as a malfunction of the mind that can increase physical disease. Worrying is helpful only as a first reaction to identify a problem. Incessant worry taxes the mind, and the "worry loop" becomes so consuming that you lose your power to engage in adequate problem-solving.

Expressing concern and engaging in problem-solving is productive. The key to effective and productive behavior is to only accept appropriate responsibility. Other people also have responsibilities, and you are not fully responsible for everything. You can make your contributions. You cannot control the total outcome. Worry and guilt are limiting behaviors. You want to be responsible, but within limits. Worry and guilt can be controlled by recognizing the limits of what you are able to accomplish.

Controlling the use of apologies is also an issue in loss of power. Women, with their nurturing behaviors, often express concern with "I am sorry." Expressions of concern must be expressed carefully. Your concern may be perceived as either "rubbing it in," or interpreted as though you contributed to the problem. Unfortunately, saying, "I am sorry" can be misinterpreted as placing yourself in a one-down position of fault that robs you of your power. Avoid apologies and express concern without the use of the "I" pronoun. You need to step back and be a responsible individual, but not the over-responsible one.

Counter Thoughts

1. Problems are a natural part of living.
2. I want to spend my time problem-solving, not worrying.
3. I do the best I can; I need to monitor my guilt.
4. I cannot change the past, I can only move on.
5. I am responsible for my own behaviors.
6. I cannot control the full outcome.

POWER ROBBER #9

I must keep the peace and not make waves.

Messages from Society

➢ Don't speak unless you are spoken to.

➢ Be respectful—don't contradict.

➢ Girls should be seen and not heard.

➢ Don't be a troublemaker.

Questions to Ask Yourself

— Do you view yourself as a peacemaker?

— Do you have difficulty "speaking out"?

— Do you have difficulty taking initiative?

— Is it difficult for you to express a different point of view?

— Do you prefer to be in the background rather than the forefront?

— Do you avoid being viewed as a wavemaker?

— Do you see being a wavemaker as being a troublemaker?

Breakfast Club Story

Laurie Gordon-Brown is a dentist who has been an elected leader in the Florida dental community. As the Women of Wisdom Power Breakfast Group was selecting their personal power-robbing stories, Laurie surprised us by selecting this one. Despite her leadership qualities and leadership positions, Laurie discussed how, as the youngest in her family, she always avoided confrontation and did not want to create any family waves.

During her dental school days, Laurie was less vocal and avoided protesting differential performance expectations. As she continued on in her career, she became active in dental politics as the first woman president of the South Broward Dental Society, a delegate to the

Florida Dental Association, and the editor of the East Coast Dental Society Newsletter. Even in these positions of leadership, Laurie, initially, avoided some of the divisive issues within the dental society.

Laurie discussed the political intricacies of dental politics. As a perceptive woman, she often had different viewpoints and insights. However, at times, her avoidance of confrontation causes her to withhold commentary. Laurie contributes time, work, and dedication. However, it is a loss to the organizations that her full input as a change agent, often, is stifled.

Overview

Females have always had the role of the peacemaker. The difficulty being a peacemaker is that you seek agreement. Often, if your focus is maintaining agreement, you lose the opportunity of asking provocative questions. If you are afraid of making waves, it undermines your ability to make a strong impression. The idea of women needing to suppress themselves has even been popularized in the media with the image of Edith and Archie Bunker. Archie encouraged Edith to "stifle herself." Stifling yourself is an extremely power-draining behavior. Camille Paglia states in her groundbreaking book *Vamps and Tramps*, "The 'nice' girl with her soft, sanitized speech and decorous manners, had to go."

Messages to avoid contrary opinions have been communicated to women for over two hundred years. You now have to remind yourself that avoiding wavemaking truncates growth. The growth truncation takes place when peacefulness at all costs, represses constructive conflict. Using constructive conflict allows you to challenge traditional viewpoints and respond to change more effectively. Particularly, in these changing times, active involvment as a change agent is necessary.

Strong influences often prevent women from being wavemakers. Characterizing a woman as a "bitch" is often society's attempt to keep women in line. Additionally, women often resist "speaking out," fearful of retribution, rather than mere stage fright. During the Puritan witch hunts, an expression of contrary opinions could cost women their lives.

In early American history, women who spoke up would be publicly chastised for such assertiveness. In this way, the subtle socialization message of controlling women's verbalizations became engrained in society.

Deborah Tannen notes in her book *You Just Don't Understand* that women often engage in assenting behaviors that mask their expertise and causes them to avoid mobilizing their talents as a source of power. Top leadership requires decisiveness and "making waves." Managers, entrepreneurs, community leaders, and parents all need to respond to change with creativity and input. You want your input to be included in the information used for decision-making. Women frequently have a unique perspective that enhances decisions. Allow your input to be heard. Make waves!

Counter Thoughts

1. New viewpoints are to be encouraged, not stifled.
2. Having a different opinion is not adversarial.
3. I can be considerate and respectful while still expressing my opinion.
4. Expressing an opinion and taking a stand is necessary for women's wisdom to have an impact.
5. All conflict is not to be avoided.
6. Constructive conflict allows forward momentum.
7. Varying perspectives from women and men enhance decisions.

POWER ROBBER #10

I must wait to be recognized for my achievements.

Messages from Society

➤ It is not appropriate for women to brag.

➤ Be careful to wait your turn.

➤ Ladies don't draw attention to themselves.

➤ Don't be too smart; you will create problems.

➤ Give credit to others before yourself.

Questions to Ask Yourself

—— Do you expect that recognition will only come as a result of fine work?

—— Do you rely on the awareness of others to recognize your achievements?

—— Do you feel uncomfortable sharing a success story?

—— Do you feel it is bragging to talk about your accomplishments?

—— Do you compliment others without recognizing your achievements?

—— When you are complimented, do you minimize your achievements?

Karen's Story

Karen is an outstanding regional manager who has been a manager for over nine years. Presently Karen manages a sales team of sixty plus salespersons. Her office is located in Fort Lauderdale, and the corporate headquarters are in Miami. Despite her achievements, Karen has difficulty calling attention to the outcomes of her sales team. Karen stated, "I don't call up and tell the vice-president my latest corporate sale." As a result, Karen has noticed a consistent pattern of other managers being recognized and compensated to a greater degree, due to her reluctance to inform others of her accomplishments.

Karen finishes one major sales presentation and then turns her focus to the next project, without passing the details of the latest success to others. Thus, she is truncating her ability to have her compensation match her achievements. She contrasts her own behavior to the behavior of the male managers who are very willing to give a graphic description of their sales team's accomplishments. The male managers position themselves as "knights in shining armor." Karen is increasingly aware that her difficulty with calling attention to her achievements is a limiting behavior. As tenaciously as Karen closes sales with her sales team, she is still learning how to be her own advocate.

Overview

Women's subtle socialization messages are directed at diminishing their achievements. You may frequently find yourself saying, "Oh, it was nothing" or "I was just in the right place at the right time" or "It didn't take that much work" or "It was really due to the team or my boss," rather than accepting and savoring the acknowledgment and recognition. Researchers report an interesting gender difference in credit-taking behaviors. When men succeed, they take the credit fully. When men fail, they point to external variables. In contrast, when women succeed they point to external variables. When women fail, they take the full self-criticism. The gender behaviors of women and men in describing success and failure are opposite. Your externalization of credit and propensity to be self-critical robs you of joy in your accomplishments.

Women have to monitor carefully behavior called "the depressed entitlement effect." Minorities often will devalue themselves when compared to others. Many studies have indicated that devaluing achievements is a major contribution to the wage gap between the genders. Women need to move beyond self-effacing behaviors. Women need to accept credit and draw attention to their achievements. Also, women need to recognize they are no longer a minority. Women are fifty-one percent (51%) of the United States population. Women have the power of the majority in United States society.

Women have been socialized to have a low profile. Now, and in the new millennium, you need to begin to shift to a higher profile. If you do not create the visibility, there is no way for your work to be noticed and opportunities to be created. You are endowed by nature with the ability to achieve an outstanding accomplishment in a minimum of one specific area—your challenge is to identify your areas of achievement, channel your energies and abilities into these areas, and become accomplished.

Women need to develop the ability to give themselves internal credit. Developing a high tolerance of praise and accepting recognition is essential to the acquisition of positive power. If you wait to be recognized, you are in a holding pattern that is similar to waiting to be asked out on a date. This is an outdated behavior that strips you of your ability to have control over your life and take initiative. Women have to carefully monitor that they are not socialized into an environment where they feel they are entitled. You want to activate your positive power to receive acknowledgment. Letting your accomplishments be recognized is not being obnoxious or overbearing—it is taking appropriate credit. This crucial factor of accepting credit was the key in selection of a star logo design by Women of Wisdom, Inc. You need to let your "star power" shine!

Counter Thoughts

1. I am responsible for commendable work and creating opportunities for acknowledgment.
2. Calling attention to my achievements opens new opportunities.
3. Bragging and acknowledging are two different behaviors.
4. I strive to accept compliments without minimizing behaviors.
5. I am committed to appropriately accepting credit and giving credit to others.

Controlling Power Robbers

As is evident, power robbers are subtle messages of socialization that all women experience. Few messages are black and white, and avoiding polarity-thinking means you do not want to eliminate totally all of the messages. Some of the messages have important value as we interact with sensitivity and caring to others. However, the power robber messages need to be controlled. The most effective controls are through the use of the counter thoughts. Our thoughts control our beliefs, which control our actions. Thinking for women must include both situational variables and the variables of their own needs, wants, and goals. You need to ensure that your concerns are adequately represented as you engage in your daily activities. By controlling the power robbers in your life, you gain control of your fate.

It is through the control of the power robbers that you will be more internally directed. You will have greater control over your life as you direct your life from an internal center of control versus allowing others to control you. The following self-assessment test is useful for evaluating your own baseline for internal control. This psychological test was developed with approved principles of test construction by Dr. Hanna Levenson. The guidelines for interpreting your score are based on the responses of hundreds of women and men. Different percentiles are reported for women and men because significant gender differences were found in some responses. This is consistent with the gender differences that are present in female and male behaviors. The sample population of adults was a representative sample of the population. The scoring result discussions have been added. When you are finished taking this test, you will have a clearer perception on how internally directed you are and how others impact you.

Who Controls Your Fate?

The Internality, Chance, and Powerful Others Scale

Directions: Below is a series of attitude statements. Each represents a commonly held opinion. There are no right or wrong answers. You will probably agree with some items and disagree with others. Read each statement carefully. Then indicate the extent to which you agree or disagree by using the guidelines below. First impressions are usually best. Read each statement, decide if you agree or disagree and determine the strength of your opinion. Then write in the appropriate number.

> 1 = Strongly Disagree
> 2 = Disagree Somewhat
> 3 = Slightly Disagree
> 4 = Slight Agree
> 5 = Agree Somewhat
> 6 = Strongly Agree

_____ 1. Whether or not I get to be a leader depends mostly on my ability.

_____ 2. To a great extent my life is controlled by accidental happenings.

_____ 3. I feel like what happens in my life is mostly determined by powerful people.

_____ 4. Whether or not I get into a car accident depends mostly on how good a driver I am.

_____ 5. When I make plans, I am almost certain to make them work.

_____ 6. Often there is no chance of protecting my personal interests from bad luck.

_____ 7. When I get what I want, it's usually because I'm lucky.

_____ 8. Although I might have good ability, I will not be given leadership responsibility without appealing to those in positions of power.

_____ 9. How many friends I have depends on how nice a person I am.

_____ 10. I have often found that what is going to happen will happen.

_____ 11. My life is chiefly controlled by powerful others.

_____ 12. Whether or not I get into a car accident is mostly a matter of luck.

_____ 13. People like myself have very little chance of protecting our personal interests when they conflict with those of strong pressure groups.

_____ 14. It's not always wise for me to plan too far ahead because many things turn out to be a matter of good or bad fortune.

_____ 15. Getting what I want requires pleasing those people above me.

_____ 16. Whether or not I get to be a leader depends on whether I'm lucky enough to be in the right place at the right time.

_____ 17. If important people were to decide they didn't like me, I probably wouldn't make many friends.

_____ 18. I can pretty much determine what will happen in my life.

_____ 19. I am usually able to protect my personal interests.

_____ 20. Whether or not I get into a car accident depends mostly on the other driver.

_____ 21. When I get what I want, it's usually because I worked hard for it.

_____ 22. In order to have my plans work, I make sure that they fit in with the desires of people who have power over me.

_____ 23. My life is determined by my own actions.

_____ 24. It's chiefly a matter of fate whether or not I have a few friends or many friends.

Scoring Procedures

Total your scores on the test items as indicated for each category. The number that results from the sum of the test items is your raw score. Locate your raw score on the percentile columns. The percentile, corresponding to your raw score, indicates your rating in relation to the representative sample of the population. For example, a percentile score of thirty percent (30%) indicates that twenty-nine percent (29%) of the population scored lower than you and sixty-nine (69%) scored higher.

INTERNALITY: Please add together your responses to items 1, 4, 5, 9, 18, 19, 21, and 23.

Women	Men	Percentile
26	26	15
29	29	30
32	32	50
35	35	70
38	38	85

A high score on Internality reflects that you believe your behaviors make a difference and you are very alert and task oriented in your work behaviors. Internals have a greater ability to vary their strategies. Internals will stick with their winning strategy and change a losing strategy. It is interesting to note that this category yields identical responses for women and men. Women do recognize their own abilities.

POWERFUL OTHERS: Please add together your responses on items 3, 8, 11, 13, 15, 17, 20, and 22.

Women	Men	Percentile
7	9	15
10	13	30
14	17	50
18	21	70
21	25	85

A high score on the Powerful Others scale indicate that you believe that you are strongly impacted by others. You often look to others for decision-making. Gender differences are evident in this response pattern. The fascinating difference is that men responded more frequently that powerful others influenced their lives. This result may reflect the "boys network" effect of powerful men mentoring other men.

CHANCE: Please add together your responses for items 2, 6, 7, 10, 12, 14, 16, and 24.

Women	Men	Percentile
6	7	15
10	11	30
13	15	50
16	19	70
20	23	85

A high score on Chance indicates that you minimize the contributions that you can make to the direction of your life. You believe that fate or luck are strong determinants of your future. Once again, a gender difference in response patterns emerges. High percentile scores indicate that you tend to view the world as capricious at times and you look for lucky opportunities. You also may be fond of utilizing lucky symbols to increase the amount of luck in your life.

Star Points

★ Power robbers are subtle socialization messages that women receive.

★ Power robber messages are received from many sources.

★ Power robber messages are tied to female stereotypes.

★ Power robber messages need to be identified.

★ Power-robbing messages can be altered by the use of counter thought messages.

★ The greater your ability to control power robbers, the more internally centered you are in your life.

★ The greater your ability to control power robbers, the more you are able to self-validate and celebrate your talents.

★ Controlling your power robbers is the key to moving beyond the Glass Ceiling.

★ **The top ten power robbers are:**

1. If I am accommodating and pleasing, I will have many friends and a rewarding life.
2. I want to do it right and not make mistakes.
3. I obtain security in life by finding a suitable life partner.
4. I want to avoid upsetting others.
5. I need to be polite and not make direct requests.
6. I need to treat everyone equally.
7. I need to obey the rules.
8. If there is a problem, it is my fault.
9. I must keep the peace and not make waves.
10. I must wait to be recognized for my achievements.

3

Positive
Power
Lessons

*"Creative minds have always been known
to survive any kind of bad training."*
—Anna Freud, Psychoanalyst

Power Lessons

Women have surged into the workplace in record numbers, and now the working woman is the norm, not the exception. This shift in women's roles may result in confrontational situations for which you have never been trained. As you reviewed in the previous chapter, subtle socialization messages may undermine personal effectiveness and make it difficult for you to reach your goals. What would be the outcome if society gave you different lessons? What would happen if you were encouraged to develop a different belief system?

In Chapter Two, counter thoughts were used to stop power drains. In Chapter Three, affirmations are used to begin new lessons in positive power. Each of the following lessons is keyed to help you reduce the power drain of the power robber. As an example, Power Robber #1 deals with accommodating and people-pleasing behaviors, and Lesson #1 teaches you the more effective messages of limit-setting and engaging in self-care. This chapter provides opportunities to begin developing new positive power skills. Once aware of the subtle power robbers, you will find the lessons in this chapter allow you to begin imaging yourself as a powerful individual. In the words of Gloria Steinem from *Our Power as Woman:* "In order to expand our power as women, first we need to imagine our power. The imagination of change is the first step toward change."

Positive power lessons clearly are not suggestions for women to mimic men. A major theme of this book is realizing the ineffectiveness and limiting nature of mimicking men or holding males up as the ideal, referred to as androcentrism. The lessons in this chapter teach women to activate positive power and increase effectiveness. Women will exercise their positive power with their own special female wisdom to achieve their objectives and goals.

As we've discussed in earlier chapters, women too often focus on the needs of others and do not factor in their own needs. The purpose of these lessons is to create a balance. Women want to maintain consideration for others, however, they want relationships to be reciprocal relationships. Interaction with others needs to be a two-way street, not a one-way street.

The positive power lessons identified in this next section will discuss in detail each lesson for moving beyond the power robber. Questions have again been provided to help you determine whether you are already using some of these lessons. If you answer "yes" to these questions, you are already using some of these lessons in life to gain power, but you may need to focus on the questions where your answer is "no" or if you are uncertain or uncomfortable with your answer. As you learn the positive power lessons, affirmations replace the counter thoughts listed in Chapter Two. In this chapter, you are moving to the next step. In addition to countering power-robbing messages, you now begin to "power-up" with new messages to activate your positive power behaviors.

POSITIVE POWER LESSON #1

I need to set limits and engage in adequate self-care.

Questions to Ask Yourself

___ Am I at ease saying no to more than I can do?

___ Am I careful about volunteering for new tasks?

— Do I finish or make good progress in my work by the end of the day?

— Do I consider my needs for rest, health, nutrition, and exercise in my daily schedule?

— Do I give myself time to rejuvenate?

Moving Beyond

Pleasing and accommodating others can easily lead to a life of over-extension. The charming woman that is always accommodating and pleasing to others drains herself of power, and often finds herself running out of hours at the end of the day. A powerful woman values her time and recognizes both her energy limits and time limits. As the multitude of life options increase, it is important to recognize that you have limits. Sally Helgesen, in her insightful diary studies of powerful women, *The Female Advantage*, noted that the women she followed practiced deliberate pacing tactics to rejuvenate and maintain their energy and productivity.

The problem for women is that culture praises accommodating behaviors. You receive reinforcement for not disappointing others. However, positive power lies in the ability to give yourself the same kind of care that you give to others. A balance needs to exist among work intensity, exercise, adequate nutrition, socializing, and other needs. The critical balance is achieved when you remember to consider a given request before responding. Often times, you may forget to consider yourself and become "emotionally hooked" by the requesting person. It is essential to remember you have the ability to take time to choose your response. Engaging in actions based on a careful assessment of data and a consideration of your life balance is an important lesson to learn.

Barriers to appropriate limit-setting and adequate self-care are the internal "shoulds." Every time you place a "should" requirement on yourself, you need to examine the request. "Shoulds" are internal messages of obligation, rather than thoughtful decision-making of productive choices. You do not want to be pulled by a demanding list of "shoulds." Every time you use the internal self-talk of "should," ask yourself: Is this necessary? Is this productive? Is this the best use of my time?

One of the most important ways to deal with the "shoulds" is to acknowledge "shoulds" tend to be thoughts that cause you to feel obligated, and may create guilt. A helpful way of handling "shoulds" is translating the "shoulds" to "coulds." This translation allows you to recognize that you have an option. You have the option to say "yes" and you have the option to say "no". Recognizing your options is an important part of limit-setting skills.

There may be a tendency to avoid limit setting because you fear conflict. When you make a decision to do something, another activity goes undone. This often will cause conflict with someone who has a different set of priorities, however, conflict is a necessary part of living. As you assess your options, one variable to factor into your evaluation is the resistance you may receive from others.

Conflict is an intricate part of life, not a negative experience. Conflict is also the natural outgrowth of diversity in cultures, opinions, and expectations. A conflict represents an opportunity for constructive communication. Conflict brings out into the open different ways of thinking and behaving and differences in values and priorities. Conflicts challenge us to manage our lives in ways that utilize our differences for our own mutual growth and benefit.

For you to weigh all of the personal cost and benefit factors, you need to possess a clear understanding of your own priorities and make beneficial decisions. Maintaining productive behaviors means you need to take steps not to push yourself too hard. If you feel burned out, tense, or irritable, then you need to reassess and change your direction. You need to be able to cancel or to renegotiate requirements, and not be afraid of disappointing someone else. No one is keeping score and you need to be your own primary self-care agent. You are responsible for creating a tolerable and manageable life.

In order to lead a productive balanced life, you need to learn the behaviors of *healthy selfish*. Healthy selfish behaviors have the components of limit-setting and an attention to adequate self-care. Limits allow us to manage time, and attention to adequate self-care allows us to balance needs. Healthy selfish is being considerate of others while factoring in your own needs. A helpful imagery is to imagine a seesaw. Do you remember when you were a child and the fun you would have going up and down and up and down? Life as a child on a seesaw can be exhilarating, enthralling highs and lows. However, if you live your life like a seesaw, one is being constantly propelled from highs to lows in an exhausting scenario. If you imagine that same seesaw but seek to have the tasks side balanced by the play side, you create a equilibrium. This life balance allows appreciation and enjoyment of work, play, and a nurturing of self that is essential to both physical and mental health. Healthy selfish behaviors are a key investment, and the greatest gifts that you can give to yourself.

You also want to control your enthusiasm for life. As an individual interested in many activities, you probably often want to do more activities than there are hours in the day. An enthusiasm for life is a wonderful attribute. However, enthusiasm for life has to be balanced by the reality of limited hours. You need to protect your time and energy by engaging in personal planning and establishing boundaries on your willingness and enthusiasm.

You do not live a life of simplicity. You lead a life of multiplicity, which can lead to fragmentation rather than unification. Conflicting demands create a whirlwind of activity that can cause you to become uncentered. Your mindset is to see yourself as internally centered with clear limits, no matter how chaotic your life may be around you. A helpful analogy is the center of a hurricane. Although a lot of maiming debris may be floating around the center, the center itself is tranquil. Even if your life is like a hurricane, you can maintain your internal center with stabilizing guidelines of clear limits.

A barrier to maintaining consistency with limit-setting and self-care is the difficulty of saying no and disappointing someone else. The strong socialization that women receive to be pleasing and accommodating causes them to feel guilty when they establish limits and engage in healthy selfish behaviors.

The guilt feelings that a woman may experience need to be countered. It is impossible to go through life and engage in healthy selfish behaviors without feeling some level of guilt. The objective is not to eliminate guilt, but to moderate guilt and maintain the focus on healthy selfish behaviors. The key dimensions of healthy selfish behaviors are the ability to set limits in terms of others' requests and demands, maintain adequate time management, and plan adequate self-care, including exercise and nutrition. Healthy selfish behaviors are the key to discovering and keeping your emotional equilibrium and a centered calm control of your life. *A powerful woman is a healthy selfish woman.*

Can you tell where you are on the scale of healthy selfish behaviors? Do you say the words healthy selfish and feel comfortable? Is your desk drowning in unread material? Is your voicemail clogged with backup calls? Do you find yourself avoiding phone calls and contact because you have so many incomplete tasks? If this reminds you of some of your behaviors, then recognize that the lesson of healthy selfish, with limit-setting and life balanced components, is an essential lesson. Guilt may be a block to your healthy selfish behaviors, but guilt is a psychological phenomenon that must be controlled and countered. It is helpful to think of your guilt as a thermometer. Imagine a guilt thermometer range of one to ten, and that you always want to use positive power tools to lower your guilt thermometer to below five. Overcoming guilt allows healthy selfish behaviors to flourish.

Maria's Story

Maria completed her term as President of the Chamber of Commerce, and was asked to serve again on the board of directors. Maria owned her own business, was married, and had two school-aged children. During executive coaching sessions, Maria recognized that she was flattered by the offer, but admitted that she was looking forward to the freedom to attend or not attend chamber meetings. After serving on the board of directors for three years and being president for one year, she desired to redirect her energies.

However, she maintained a strong appreciation for the other member's support of her presidency and had strong allegiance to the chamber. Maria was agitated and having difficulty reaching a decision. She spoke at length of the numerous favors she had received. She was concerned that leaving the board would result in a loss of her support network. She was also concerned she would be letting down her supporters. Maria was tossing and turning at night, and sleeping poorly.

Acknowledging the contributions that she had made by utilizing healthy selfish self-talk, Maria was able to lower her guilt thermometer to a three and resign from the board. Once her decision was made, she felt an immediate internal calm and her decision was accepted by the board. At her final meeting as president, the board presented her with a lovely gift of appreciation. This was a major learning experience for Maria that being healthy selfish and setting limits did not mean she would be viewed as a "bitch." Others can be very accepting and supportive of realistic limits. Maria reports that she continues to have contact with board members and her relationships remained intact.

Affirmations

1. As I engage in adequate self-care, I maintain my energy for my life's tasks.
2. I focus on my own internal gauge of self-care and comfort.
3. I listen to my inner voice and balance my life.
4. I want to be considerate of others, not consumed by others.
5. A disappointment is not a disaster.
6. Healthy selfish behaviors allow me to be considerate of both myself and others.

POSITIVE POWER LESSON #2

I welcome mistakes as an indicator that I am pushing my limits and being all I can be.

Questions to Ask Yourself

___ Do you avoid double and triple checking your work?

___ Are you comfortable with the suggestion that you may have made a mistake?

___ Are you glad that when an error is found so you can work on the solution?

___ When you make a mistake, are you able to move forward without engaging in self-critical behaviors?

___ Do you take the opportunity to learn from your mistakes?

Moving Beyond

This is a significant mind shift from the power robber of avoiding mistakes and seeking perfectionism. The new cognitive mindset is that mistakes are a natural part of learning. John Dewey, a noted American educator, founded his educational philosophy on the concept of "learning by doing." Learning is an ongoing process in your life. Trial and error learning is often the best teacher. Difficulties challenge your talents and surmounting difficulties is very rewarding. But these rewards bring the risks of mistakes, and that can cause you to freeze in fear at your error. You need to recognize mistakes create impactful learning experiences. Oprah Winfrey stated in her commencement address at Wesleyan University, "There is no such thing as failure. Mistakes happen in your life to bring into focus more clearly who you really are."

You may react fearfully to mistakes, often replaying the mistake over and over in your mind. You also may be defensive about the mistake, and bristle if someone suggests you have made an error. These reactions consume time and energy, and are not constructive. When you view mistakes as adding valuable data to your learning curve, they have productive value.

Rather than being upset or devastated by mistakes, reward yourself for stretching yourself and moving to new areas. Mistakes become a learning experience for growth and understanding. As you develop tolerance for mistakes, you will find that you are able to function more independently and with increased confidence. You will find yourself initiating new actions.

Another valuable aspect of increasing your tolerance of mistakes is expanding your ability to handle constructive criticism. When you filter critical feedback with a positive sense of acquiring helpful information from team members, superiors, and peers, you will be successful. Integrating constructive feedback allows you to increase your productivity. Your openness to constructive criticism adds data to your learning curve. The more you learn, the more productive and creative you become.

When you are not tolerant of mistakes, your emotional response to a critical remark will be personal hurt. This will then become a personal emotional disability. A high tolerance of mistakes allows you to integrate constructive criticism and protects you from being hurt. Accepting mistakes and feedback becomes personal armor that shields you, thus, a tolerance of mistakes is necessary to become a seasoned executive.

Debbie's Story

Debbie was a forty-two-year-old married female with three high school aged children. She had been promoted to controller of a major corporation, with a history of ten plus years of employment and consistent accolades. As she assumed the position of controller of the corporation, she began to have more interaction with the board of directors. For the first time, during board of directors meetings, Debbie found herself needing to clarify and explain her investment strategies. Debbie was referred for executive coaching by her chief executive officer, a strong supporter of Debbie, who felt that her strong defensive reactions at board meetings called his promotion selection into question.

During coaching sessions, Debbie verbalized a long career of consistent success and the perception that her decisions were usually on track. She felt reproached and denigrated at the board meetings. She viewed herself as "on the spot" and under the microscope. Debbie was the first female controller of this corporation. She was angry, resentful, and felt treated unfairly.

As coaching sessions progressed, Debbie was able to see that the board of directors viewed themselves as part of her investment team. She began to consider the possibility the board was brainstorming the best investment strategies, rather than criticizing her. Once Debbie was able to shift her cognitive mindset to the board as part of her investment team, she reduced her defensiveness and began to develop a strong rapport with them. During her six-month follow-up visit, Debbie was relaxed and enjoying her new position. She also advocated for the inclusion of a female on the board. Her job performance and personal credibility had significantly increased. Debbie was now a major contributor to corporate policy.

Affirmations

1. I will engage in self-correction, not self-condemnation.
2. Corrective input from others is to be welcomed nondefensively.
3. A mistake is an opportunity for new learning.
4. If there is a mistake, I will be gentle and tolerant with myself.
5. Mistakes are part of my humanity and I refuse to condemn myself for any shortcomings or mistakes.
6. As a seeker of excellence, but not a perfectionist, I am open to direction and constructive criticism.

POSITIVE POWER LESSON #3

I create security by developing my own competencies.

Questions to Ask Yourself

___ Am I willing to accept total responsibility for my welfare?

___ Do I enjoy my relationships versus being dependent on my relationships?

___ Do I seek opportunities to develop my abilities?

___ Do I recognize my multiple competencies?

___ Do I find that my ability to be self-sufficient is an exciting prospect?

___ Do I recognize that I will always be able to locate needed resources?

Moving Beyond

Allowing yourself to focus on your own abilities and talents creates internal security. When you remain externally focused on relationships as essential to life function, you are doomed to a rollercoaster of worry and insecurity. Women have strong needs for affiliation which is important, but the one who you need to rely on is yourself. Self-reliance and self-sufficiency are keys to maintaining an adequate equilibrium and being in charge of your life.

Security in life stems from being able to have varied abilities and multiple skills as your core competencies. As a competent individual, you recognize and develop your talents. You have the ability to earn a living and you have the ability to reachout to tap needed resources. Your security stems from the recognition of your strengths, your talents, and your abilities. Being able to acknowledge and recognize your talents and abilities also allows you to acknowledge your own successes.

Confident individuals are constantly focusing on building their strengths and widening their core competencies while decreasing their limitations. Recognizing and accepting the personal responsibility for your economic, emotional, and social life, brings a motivating freedom to expand your skills. You become committed to the expansion of your core competencies to create your preferred lifestyle. Self-sufficiency and self-reliance do not limit your ability to enjoy relationships, recognize the importance of interpersonal interaction, and treasure loved ones. Your own internal security allows you to enjoy people for what they add to your life, rather than rely on others. Interpersonal relationships become more joyous and open without hidden agendas of dependency.

The security you obtain in life is through your own efforts. Security is when you have effective life strategies and the ability to traverse life with confidence, multiple strategies, and resources through your core competencies.

Breanna's Story

Breanna entered therapy coping with the end of a thirteen-year monogamous, lesbian relationship. Breanna was a woman in her late forties who was supported by her partner, not only emotionally, but also as an employee in her lover's business. Throughout the years of their relationship, Breanna was not a stockholder in the company—she was an employee. When her lover elected to end the relationship and began a relationship with another female, Breanna was devastated. Breanna had built her security and her future totally around her lover's business and the expectation that the relationship would be lifelong.

Breanna reported a fearfulness for her future. She was confused, angry, and hurt. During initial sessions, her words became garbled with her tears. She had difficulty envisioning a future. She stated, "I feel hopeless and inept. I am lost." During treatment, Breanna was able to recognize that her lover possessed the technical skills for the computer repair business. However, the management, customer service, scheduling function, financial functions, and employee supervision were totally managed by Breanna. As she identified her own core competencies, she accepted the reality of being self-sufficient.

Only then was Breanna able to proactively make plans for her future. At the time of discharge from therapy, Breanna was starting a business of her own with a partner and looking forward to her own entrepreneurial enterprise. Although sad, she was moving forward with her own life plans.

Affirmations

1. My relationships are only a portion of my life, and I am independently capable.
2. I can set meaningful goals that give direction to my life.
3. I can choose what I want and go after it.
4. I can ask for help when I need it.
5. I can be flexible and persistent in pursuing my goals.
6. I recognize and develop my talents.

POSITIVE POWER LESSON #4

I seek the respect of others and recognize that some people will be uncomfortable around me.

Questions to Ask Yourself

___ Are you able to tolerate an uncomfortable feeling?

___ Are you able to consistently and credibly state your position?

___ Do you value being respected more than being popular?

___ Can you disagree with someone and not have it contaminate the relationship?

___ Can you tolerate being questioned by others without becoming defensive and taking it personally?

Moving Beyond

As you monitor your behaviors of over-responsibility, you learn to recognize that you are responsible only for your own behaviors. You begin to be less concerned with other people's reactions and more concerned with maintaining the clarity of your own beliefs, values, and behaviors. Personal credibility and respect become valued more than being a "nice girl" that never upsets anyone.

Life is not an endless popularity contest, but a balance of differing needs and responsibilities. You become aware that there are many different perspectives and viewpoints. The most important behaviors are to be credible and respectful of others' opinions. However, being respectful of other perspectives does not mean that you have to always defer to others. A healthy relationship will be able to tolerate constructive disagreement. Psychological research demonstrates that even in romantic relationships, intimacy requires a certain amount of conflict.

Since disagreements and different levels of conflict are an inevitable part of life, the ability to stand your ground while respecting others' perspectives is essential. You also need to have the ability to verbalize your own position and feelings with clarity, as negotiation involves clear understandings by all parties. As you experience disagreements in life, they do not have to be win-lose encounters, but can be negotiated compromises. Often a healthy respect for different viewpoints allows all viewpoints to be given credence in either personal or business negotiations. Conflict resolution skills focus on an open exchange of information and the willingness to thoroughly examine all viewpoints to reach agreement or consensus.

Not only must women be able to tolerate and discuss different viewpoints, women need to recognize that even though they are entering the workforce in large numbers, women are still an anomaly in many settings. In particular, executive women are still in the process of being pioneers, and men do not yet have the routine familiarity with women in executive settings. As a result, your gender in and of itself may cause some discomfort for others, but you need to avoid responding to others' discomfort personally. Often, interpersonal discomfort can be an open door for discussion, and uncomfortable interpersonal interactions can be viewed as a challenge to resolve the discomfort and develop a mutually respectful rapport. The lesson is to shift your focus from a concern with others' feelings, over which you have no control, and to a focus on conducting yourself in a manner that promotes respect.

Molly's Story

Molly was a twenty-eight-year-old, attractive, divorced woman who had rapidly risen in the ranks of a telecommunications company. Molly had an outstanding sales performance record and was promoted to regional manager. This was Molly's first management position. She was referred for managerial coaching by the national sales manager. When I first met Molly, her charming manner, sharp wit, and deferential behaviors were disarming. During coaching sessions, Molly had great difficulty in expressing her opinions clearly. If I in any way would question her position, she would immediately shift her position to what she anticipated was my opinion.

Molly was an adept chameleon with her antenna constantly adjusting her viewpoints to her audience. Molly's keen insight into others' behaviors and her ability to mirror their needs was an exceptional skill as a salesperson. However, as a regional sales manager it was a problem for Molly to continue these behaviors, as she was not providing adequate leadership or direction to the sales staff.

During coaching sessions, Molly was able to recognize that the constant behaviors of agreement prevented her from developing a leadership style to manage her region. It took a considerable amount of time for Molly to tolerate disagreements, maintain a consistent leadership stance, and be open to disagreements among her sales staff, while providing clear direction. When the coaching sessions ended, Molly commented, "Becoming an effective manager was more difficult than creating a million dollars in sales."

Affirmations

1. Being respected by others is more important than being liked.
2. Disagreements are a healthy exchange of different viewpoints.
3. Constructive conflict can strengthen relationships.
4. As an executive woman, I need to be tolerant of male colleagues who are still adjusting to the changes in the workforce.
5. My goal is to be effective and productive.

POSITIVE POWER LESSON #5

I need to ask for what I want to reach my goals.

Questions to Ask Yourself

___ Do you assume full responsibility for creating opportunity in your life?

___ Do you no longer need to ask permission to make requests?

___ Are you comfortable with making direct requests?

___ Do you know what you want?

___ Do you have a life strategy?

Moving Beyond

The new training required to go beyond being polite and asking permission is for you to assume personal responsibility for creating what you want in life. The assumption of personal responsibility makes you the designer and sculptor of your life. You assume a positive power position to control the outcome of your life. No longer will you be asking permission or depending on others to allow you opportunities that you need. Instead, you will voice your requests directly. You will become an activist creating opportunities as the moments arise.

Asking directly for what you want first requires that you know what you want. Often women have been so encouraged to concentrate on the needs and desires of others, that they have been diverted from identifying their own goals. Given women's powerful socialization training, this "other focus" is understandable. You now need to develop a strong internal focus. This internal focus will allow you to identify your own personal goals and needs. Once you have completed the identification process, you then begin to develop and implement a plan to reach your goals.

Along the way you will also shed, much like a butterfly sheds its cocoon, the past behaviors of permission-asking and indirectness. As you identify and create new paths of opportunity in your life, you will find the shortest route between two places on the path is always the most direct route. Your focus is to be direct, expedient, and to create opportunities. You shed the indirectness and the expectation of someone else taking care of you, and assume responsibilities while creating opportunities.

Anna's Story

Anna is a twenty-five-year-old engineering graduate of a highly ranked college. Anna was referred for executive coaching by a head-hunter whom she had approached to circulate her resume for a managerial position. Anna was the youngest of three children with two older brothers. Throughout her life, her brothers had been protective and encouraging. Anna relied on the advice of her brothers when she selected her college, chose her first job, and selected a headhunter. For the first time in her life she now was faced with the dilemma of independently identifying the "next step" in her life.

During coaching sessions, Anna presented a philosophical approach to life. She believed that life would unfold with the right opportunities arising at the right time. She had never conceptualized the behavior of assuming responsibility for clear goals and developing a strategy to meet those goals.

After the initial coaching session, follow-up sessions were held bi-monthly to aid in maintaining her momentum toward the goals she started to identify in sessions. The decision-making process for directing her own life was a new path for Anna. She stated, "I was frightened to set a clear goal. I didn't know where to start."

At an eighteen-month follow-up, Anna was actively participating in identifying goals, strategizing, utilizing resources, and actively seeking opportunities. She had made a significant job change, increased her salary base by eight thousand dollars, and became the manager of a ten-employee department. Anna's comment during our last follow-up session was, "Once my plan was in place, I was able to create a momentum that was exciting. I can remember that lost feeling when I first entered your office, feeling that I had no clear direction. Becoming more self-directed has been a freeing experience for me."

Affirmations

1. People cannot read my mind; I must know what I want.
2. I want to maximize the possibility of reaching my goals.
3. I am responsible for getting what I need.
4. If I ask directly, I increase the possibility of having my request fulfilled.
5. By asking clearly and directly, I am an effective communicator.
6. I need to consistently plan and reassess my life goals.
7. I will seize opportunities to reach my goals.

POSITIVE POWER LESSON #6

I need to be discriminating in my interactions with others.

Questions to Ask Yourself

____ Do you carefully consider your resources before volunteering for a committee?

____ Do you think carefully before automatically accepting projects?

____ Do you select among invitations?

____ Do you take time to evaluate the reciprocity of relationships?

____ Have you developed a criteria for the type of collegial support that you need to advance toward your goals?

Moving Beyond

Time and energies are limited. As a consequence, it is important for you to be highly discriminating in your interactions with others. The best investments of time and energy are when you make selections which bring benefits to your life. By making differential assessments, you are able to establish your own priorities and meet your own goals. If you are constantly available and constantly concerned about spreading yourself equally among relationships, you will not have the focus and time to obtain your goals. It is also important to have a support team. Different people will mesh differently with other people, and offer different but complementary skills and strengths to your support team. As part of your positive power usage, you want to identify mutual alliances that will enhance your life.

Connectedness to others is important. Numerous psychological studies have demonstrated that human interaction is essential to the quality of life. Even as an infant, the absence of the human touch and interaction can result in a "failure to thrive." Human interactions are precious and to be treasured. As our time is limited, it is important to be discriminating in your choice of alliances. You want to ally yourself with people who are life-enhancing and support you. You act powerfully when you take the time to assess your relationships and ensure adequate mutual reciprocity exists before you continue the relationship. Discriminating behaviors are essential to maintain your quality of life.

Nan's Story

Nan was a talented artist and a single mother with two teenage girls. When Nan entered therapy, she was focused on developing her independent business and would, no matter what the size of the project, put a great deal of energy into perfecting each drawing. Nan's artistic skills ranged from drawing layouts for architects, to creative *trompe l'oeils* for walls and ceilings, and painting stunning canvasses. Despite her considerable talents, she often found herself experiencing severe financial difficulties. Her financial hardships often contributed to Nan's depressive symptoms. Nan frequently found herself crying, feeling despair, being overwhelmed, experiencing sleep disruptions, and feeling hopeless.

During therapy, Nan verbalized her desire to treat all of her clients equally. She did not consider economic parameters, and would put energies into her work according to her own standards. She rarely stopped to calculate the amount of hours she invested in a project in relation to the amount of money that she was paid. Nan was more focused on the caliber of her work than on the reimbursement that she received—she never considered the level of reciprocity she achieved in her client relationships. As therapy progressed, Nan began to see that she was being self-destructive. Her obsession with treating every job equally was limiting the amount of time that she had available for her daughters, emotionally exhausting her, and placing her in major financial jeopardy.

Finally, she realized that she needed to make a significant change in her behaviors. Once Nan began to discriminate in terms of what work could be produced in the most time efficient manner for the most financial gain, she was able to selectively accept or reject work. Slowly, Nan started to work smarter, rather than harder, with new tools of discrimination. The more her discriminating behaviors increased, the more her depressive symptoms decreased. As emotional and financial pressure lessened, Nan stated, "I was creating my own stress. I never stopped to consider my options. I was afraid more work wouldn't be there and accepted everything. Life is beginning to be fun."

Affirmations

1. The more discriminating I am, the quicker I will reach my goals.
2. Compatible colleagues are important for my support team.
3. I must carefully invest my time.
4. I must wisely invest my physical and emotional energies.
5. I make discriminating use of time and energy to increase my quality of living.
6. By being discriminating, I have adequate time for self-care.
7. By being discriminating, I have adequate time for the people who are most important to me.
8. I develop alliances that benefit me.

POSITIVE POWER LESSON #7

I need to understand the rules and be flexible.

Questions to Ask Yourself

__ Do you reevaluate policies and procedures on a regular basis?

__ Do you allow exceptions to the rules?

__ Do you take the time to flex a policy when needed?

__ Are you comfortable challenging rules that appear inappropriate?

__ Is it more important for you to solve the problem rather than follow the rules?

Moving Beyond

The world would be chaotic if rules were not present. However, a respect for the rules does not preclude the need for flexibility with using the rules. At times, challenging a rule may be appropriate. Rules generally are broad strokes that cannot cover every possible situation. Each situation demands a close examination of the rules, and may require some flexing of the rules. In order to be effective you have to possess the flexibility to modify a response. Flexibility cannot be created when you have blind obedience to rules. The world is not made up of black and white rules. You have to be astute in your application of rules and understand that there will always be some exceptions. You want to be sensitive to individual cases and not sabotage yourself or alienate others by a blind adherence to rules.

Additionally, defined rules are not the exclusive guidelines. In many organizations, there exists a "shadow organization" or an informal power line. Understanding informal power and the presence of unwritten rules are essential to effective functioning. Both written rules and unwritten rules need to be evaluated before deciding a course of action.

To be a true leader you need to be able to go beyond the rules or even create a new set of rules. Innovative flexibility is required to develop new visions and activate change. This is particularly crucial for women as they are challenged to utilize their power and their wisdom to reshape the world.

Violet's Story

Violet was referred for executive coaching by the executive vice president of a corporation. Violet had been consistently rated a top manager, but recently there were numerous complaints. As the coaching sessions progressed, Violet began to discuss how difficult it was to consistently apply corporate policies and procedures. It soon became obvious that Violet was conscientious and followed office policy "to the letter." During the ten years that Violet had been director of human resources, the employee composition had changed dramatically. The diverse employee population and the needs of the population were not met by the outdated office procedure and rules. Violet's strong allegiance to the rules caused her to not have the ability to step back, recognize the changes in the employee population, be flexible to challenge some of the rules and policies, and be an agent of change.

As coaching continued, Violet was able to become less defensive and recognize that she was caught in a trap of applying outdated policies and procedures. During coaching sessions, Violet was able to proactively plan strategies to create an employee supervisor committee to recommend revisions to office policies and procedures. A six-month follow-up call to the corporation noted significant policy changes were made, and, furthermore, the levels of complaints had significantly declined.

Violet called a month later for a "booster session." Patients are encouraged to return to coaching on their own initiative, and these sessions are called "booster sessions." During her next session, she talked at length of how the experience at work had also influenced her home life. "I never realized that taking care of everything according to my perceptions was a problem. As I began to engage at home in the information-gathering dialogues that I learned in coaching sessions, resentments from my family bubbled over. The shift to coordinating versus running everything has been difficult. The best benefit is now, I get hugs, not hostility."

Affirmations

1. I recognize that rules may become outdated.
2. I respect the rules but know, at times, rules need to be challenged.
3. I value my ability to be flexible and conduct a situational analysis.
4. I have the ability to question rules and make needed changes.
5. People are more important than rules.
6. I consider both the written and unwritten rules in my decision-making.
7. I can be a change agent to establish new rules.

POSITIVE POWER LESSON #8

I need to engage in positive self-talk and monitor over-responsibility.

Questions to Ask Yourself

___ Do you assess your mistakes to learn from them rather than being critical of yourself?

___ Do you rarely berate yourself?

___ Do you take time to engage in positive self-talk?

___ Do you separate what you are responsible for from others' responsibilities?

___ Are you committed to generating a positivity in your life?

___ Do you spend time in daily positive "mindercise?"

Moving Beyond

Over-responsibility is a trap that causes you to engage in self-blame and to feel guilty when problems emerge, problems for which you may not have responsibility or solutions. Assuming responsibility is important, but over-assuming responsibility for matters beyond your control can lead to increasing guilt. Guilt and worry fuel negative self-talk. Negative self-talk creates a self-defeating cycle, which undermines effectiveness and the utilization of positive power. Positive self-talk is a counter to guilt and worry, and needs to become a daily behavior coupled with a watchful eye on assuming responsibilities. Positive self-talk allows you to achieve your goals and generates good feelings. Positive self-talk involves talking to yourself about past successes, how you overcame obstacles and how you felt good. Positive talking can also encompass positive imaging. You want to imagine yourself achieving your goals. Imaging and visioning become programmers of your mind. As you program your mind with positives, you help to manage your mind's productions.

We talk to ourselves continuously, our brains are perpetually active, and our inner statements have the ability to affect us dramatically. In order to unleash your positive power, you want to be sure that you are constantly encouraging yourself with self-celebrating thoughts. By creating a constant stream of positive self-talk, you overcome discouraging messages.

Self-talk is not just comprised of random words. Self-talk impacts our ability to perform and creates our emotions. Positive self-talk generates beliefs in yourself. An easy way to remember this is to consider the phrase, "To Be The First." Take the first letter of each word, T-B-T-F: Thoughts, (T), lead to beliefs, (B), generating additional thoughts, (T), which create your feelings, (F). It is very important to recognize that you create the reality of your world by your self-talk.

Since self-talk is so vital to both mental and physical health, you want to engage in daily "mindercise." Part of your "mindercise" is to study the environment, gather information, and challenge your mind. Additional "mindercise" is to have a program of daily meditating or reading an affirmation book to continue to generate a positive, internal, self-talk focus. This proactive self-talk focus is essential to maintaining your emotional equilibrium. Positive self-talk also facilitates the release of endorphins in your system. Endorphins help you maintain the resiliency of your immune system and maintain both your physical health and your psychological health.

Not only is self-talk important, it is also imperative to know that you are only responsible for your own actions. Further, you do the best you can do at the moment with the information you have. You want to avoid the phenomena of " second guessing" yourself and criticizing yourself for past behaviors. Remember, when you assess yourself backward, you include new pieces of data which you did not possess at the time of your decision. The past is important, we must remember, because we learn from our past, but the most important focus is the present. The seventy percent (70%) rule is an effective guideline to building and sustaining your positive power. Seventy percent (70%) of your thoughts and energy needs to be anchored in the present. Twenty percent (20%) needs to be anchored in the past, because the past provides a database of learning experiences. Ten percent (10%) remains anchored in the future because we want to set goals. Since goals are constantly reassessed in a rapidly changing environment, you must use your ten percent (10%) to keep the goals fresh and in your sights. Still, your greatest energy needs to be focused on the seventy percent (70%) in the present, since you can readily impact the present, but cannot change the past. Think of the present as a birthday gift to be unwrapped and enjoyed. "Mindercise" with a present focus builds your positive power.

Barbara's Story

Barbara was thirty-seven-years-old, and an entrepreneur. She was a creative woman who developed a highly successful new software application for her industry. She was referred to me by an executive client who was concerned that Barbara was slipping into a depression. On meeting Barbara, her eyes darted around the room, she hung her head forward and it was difficult to obtain eye contact. Her agitation was evident because her hands were trembling. Barbara began the session by telling me how sorry she was that she was five minutes late, how terrible a day she was having due to yelling at an employee, and to pardon her appearance because she got caught in a rainstorm and her clothes were wrinkled. She worried about sitting on the couch and leaving a water stain. She forgot her checkbook and apologized for her oversight at least six times. The checkbook apologies continued despite the fact that our office accepted charge cards and payment was not an issue. Clearly, Barbara was a master at negative self-talk.

Not only was Barbara engaging in negative verbal statements, but her internal self-critic was even more extreme. As the sessions progressed, I asked Barbara to tally the number of negative statements that she made per hour. After one week of taking daily tallies, Barbara was averaging forty-two negative statements every thirty-minute period. A large percentage of her statements were self-berating for others' activities, and were not directly related to her own behavior.

The data-gathering of her negative self-talk was an eye opener for Barbara. Barbara had a delightful sense of humor and one of the clinical interventions was a thought-stopping device. To assist Barbara in her negative self-talk statements, she put a rubberband around her wrist that she would snap every time she caught herself in either an internal or external negative self-statement. The first week that she began utilizing this technique, Barbara had to wear sweaters so she would not have welts on her arms. Since my clinical practice is located in south Florida, she told her employee staff, she was testing a special new deodorant and needed to wear the sweaters to make sure that she was sweating appropriately. I am not sure whether the employees believed her deodorant testing story, however, Barbara made significant progress in reducing her negative self-talk. She appropriately limited her perceptions of responsibility, and increased her positive self-talk.

Two years later, Barbara called for a coaching session. When Barbara arrived in my office, the difference in her appearance was startling. She maintained excellent eye contact, confidently entered the room, and possessed an engaging charisma. A larger company had recently acquired Barbara's company, and she had returned for coaching assistance to plan her next career challenge.

Affirmations

1. Remember the wisdom of Eleanor Roosevelt: No one can make you feel inferior without your consent.
2. I am a worthwhile person.
3. I can do anything I set my mind to.
4. I recognize that my thoughts create my feelings.
5. I affirm myself daily.
6. I am the captain of my own cheerleading team.
7. I am committed to liking myself and accepting myself.
8. Attitude is important and my attitude is that I see the glass as half full.
9. I engage in daily "mindercise" and daily physical exercise.

POSITIVE POWER LESSON #9

I want to make waves and be a change catalyst.

Questions to Ask Yourself

___ Do you create opportunities to take the initiative?

___ Do you enjoy being a pivotal member of an organization?

___ Do you view yourself as having unique perspectives that will be of major benefit to an organization?

___ Are you willing to take a stand that is different than others in the management team?

___ Are you able to develop your own unique vision and goals for the organization?

Moving Beyond

Talent inspires productivity. Releasing your talents contributes to your organization's growth and your expression of positive power. Stifling yourself through fear of being considered a "bitch," limits your ability to contribute and to achieve, while robbing the organization of your valuable talents. As a talented individual, do not stand on the sidelines and be a spectator. Rather, you jump into the act and get involved. Take off your power brakes, speak out, and seize the initiative.

Initiative occurs with an overpowering urge for action, and is crucial to forward momentum. When you are an initiator, you become a pivotal person. Group performance pivots around action people. Thus, when you take the initiative and speak out, you have the ability to be viewed as a seasoned player whose comments are worthy of consideration. This is a new lesson for women to learn. Women have been socialized to defer, not lead.

Leadership and initiative allow you to become a change agent. Women with their unique ways of knowing, and their considerable talents have much to contribute to both their own businesses as entrepreneurs and to corporate cultures as executives. The Federal Glass Ceiling Commission discussed in detail the need to tap the considerable talents of women for businesses to remain competitive in the new global economy. Failure to utilize forty-six percent (46%) of the workforce talent, by excluding women's contributions, will greatly affect the bottomline and business growth will be truncated.

Women have much to offer as substantial change agents. As the new millennium approaches, women are poised at a historical point, primed with the critical mass of numbers, to be agents of transformtion. Women have been in the business pipeline long enough to move beyond the Glass Ceiling and to take positions at the helm. When one is at the helm as a valued senior manager, you speak the truth about business realities and make important contributions to the directions of business.

Research demonstrates that executive women in the higher ranks and those who own their own companies are more likely to speak the truth about business realities, make the necessary waves, and accomplish needed changes. Women who conform to the norm and avoid the initiative are not utilizing the full spectrum of their abilities. Moreover, women with their unique ways of knowing, have perceptive abilities different from men, and expressing these unique insights will assist the change process.

As you learn to be out in front and to take initiative, you express your unique perspectives, and are a change agent. As a catalyst of change, you will also find that your alliances will strengthen. Others are drawn to individuals who posses a vision and are leading the company in a strong direction. Pat Moran, as CEO of JM Family Enterprises, reached her position through her abilities to inspire associates and develop corporate strategies. Pat's ability to be a visionary for her corporation and take appropriate initiatives are her hallmark as an outstanding executive. Pat's visions for the corporation attract talented women to join her team, as for example, Holly C. Giertz.

Breakfast Club Story

Holly C. Giertz, Vice President for JM&A Group, a JM Family Enterprises, Inc. company, has not only made multiple waves in her life, but has ridden many as well. As a young surfer, Holly reached the highest status possible with the Eastern Surfing Association and learned a valuable lesson that all women need to learn: you need to be in the right position to ride the waves. In order to reach the optimum position, you must take the initiative and be comfortable with being a change agent.

Holly's ability to take initiative has been a major key to her success. At sixteen, Holly moved out of her home and attended high school during the day and worked as an overseas telephone operator from 11:00 at night until 7:00 in the morning, as she focused on becoming economically self-sufficient. At age eighteen, Holly became pregnant. When she found her husband with her best friend, she left Florida with her son and a one-way ticket to Colorado, not knowing anyone at the other end. Holly took the initiative to relocate herself with minimal education and a one-and-a-half-year-old child. But after one year, she engaged in a cost-benefit analysis and returned to Florida. When she returned, she worked two jobs, went to school at night and turned to welfare and food stamps for further support. Once again, Holly showed her resiliency. She completed a real estate course and subsequently reached a million dollars in sales. Holly was the youngest real estate broker in Jacksonville Beach, Florida, and, later opened her own real estate office.

After a divorce, Holly's next career was with Citicorp in south Florida. When she was considered for her first managerial position, she was told she could not be a manager as a divorced, single mother. Holly prepared a presentation stating why *she* would be the best manager for the job. She, once again, showed the power of initiative and received the promotion. During Holly's twelve years at Citicorp, she received numerous accolades and was promoted eight times. Holly continued to take initiative in her life to seize new opportunities and determined that it was time to transition outside of Citicorp. As she explored options, Holly identified

JM Family Enterprises as a corporation without a Glass Ceiling. She slowly developed a relationship with the corporation over a three-year period and joined the company in 1996. Through Holly's initiatives, she once again reached her goal. After demonstrating impressive abilities and building credibility within the corporation, Holly's ability to reshape the environment took her from manager, to director, to vice-president within a short two-year period. Clearly, initiative can make a difference in reaching your goals.

Affirmations

1. I have a unique perspective that needs to be expressed.
2. Being a change agent adds meaning to my life.
3. I enjoy the challenge of moving an organization in new directions.
4. As a change agent, I maintain crucial alliances.
5. Taking initiative is crucial to reaching my goals.
6. Taking initiative allows me to shape the organization toward my vision.

POSITIVE POWER LESSON #10

I acknowledge my accomplishments and seek appropriate recognition.

Questions to Ask Yourself

____ Do you acknowledge your significant contributions to a project?

____ Do you create opportunities for broadening your achievements by expanding your skills?

____ Do you accept acknowledgments gracefully without diminishing them?

____ Do you seek opportunities to have your achievements communicated?

Moving Beyond

Prior messages to have a low profile and stay in the background counteract your ability to obtain recognition and acknowledgment for your accomplishments. Obtaining recognition is necessary to create new opportunities. Having positive power and handling power with the comfort level of a second skin requires that you receive acknowledgments with comfort. In addition, you need to create a strong record of your achievements and leadership to enable you to move even further forward.

Acknowledging accomplishments and seeking appropriate avenues for recognition are necessary steps in climbing the ladder of success. Identifying appropriate avenues to seek recognition requires that you be a strategic listener. You always want to engage in active listening, possess a good memory for names (or find a recall tool), and be viewed as considerate and credible. Seeking acknowledgment is not being egotistical, but rather shows respect and appreciation for yourself and others. You followup your strategic listening with a speedy response with suggestions. You send thank-you notes with an exchange of ideas. You develop a deep down feeling of your own self-worth and you possess a positive self-image. You take pride in what you are doing, and what you are accomplishing.

A key way to gaining recognition is to have strong credibility. Your word is your bond. Your recognition will increase when you make requests that you can follow through on, make a promise that you keep, and make decisions that you support. As you stockpile your accomplishments and raise your profile in the organization, you increase your positive power position. You, then, will be viewed as a rainmaker. In a rainmaker position, you shape policy and contribute to the organization's vision and bottomline.

June's Story

June was a buyer for a major retail store. During a difficult transition project with computers, June would often work sixteen to eighteen hours per day. Additionally, she coached, mentored, and trained a junior colleague in completing his projects. During this time, June was so involved in being conscientious and completing all of her tasks, that she had minimal contact with her managers. Moreover, when she did attempt to have contact with her managers, she found herself being excluded. June was the supervisor for a number of field representatives. Much to her chagrin, she found out that meetings were being held with her staff, her manager, and the junior colleague, and she was being excluded. The final straw for June was when she was transferred to another store, subsequently received a poor evaluation, whereas her junior male colleague received a major raise and was promoted.

June, up to this point, had not paid sufficient attention to having upper management recognize her work performance. As a salaried employee, upper management had no tracking mechanism for her outstanding efforts. Her manager was not aware of the number of hours she worked or her contribution to her junior colleague's projects. During executive coaching sessions, June appropriately contacted the human resources department, grieved her evaluation, and subsequently had meetings with higher levels of management. Only then was there an awareness of the significant contributions that she had made. Additionally, this retail corporation is a company that prides itself on its mentoring of women. In doing my research for the book, I found it ironic to have this corporation pay lipservice to a philosophy that they were unable to implement in reality.

After the grievance process, June began to be more conscious of the "recognition factor." She documented her job performance and initiated meetings with her manager. Her initiatives resulted in a letter of commendation and a bonus. In her last session, June stated, "I will never be invisible again. I recognize that communicating your achievements is as important as the achievement itself."

Affirmations

1. Acknowledgments are not boasting.
2. Recognition creates new opportunities.
3. "Tooting my own horn" is necessary for advancement.
4. When I acknowledge my achievements, I can also acknowledge others' achievements and strengthen my alliances.
5. I seek opportunities to be recognized.
6. I recognize that by being acknowledged I position myself as a leader.

Activating the Lessons

In the prior chapter, you raised your awareness of subtle power drains. This chapter began the development of new lessons and new skills. Women have many challenges ahead of them. You are challenged to tap into the reservoir of power that rests within you. Do not let fear stand in your way. You can overcome fear and activate your new positive power skills. Althea Horner, in her insightful book, *The Wish for Power and the Fear of Having It*, noted, "Real power transcends the whim of chance of fortune, enabling the individual to persevere and even triumph through adversity." Positive power skills are your keys to activating the doors of increased opportunity.

Star Points

★ Positive power lessons increase personal effectiveness.

★ Positive power skills are utilized with the wisdom of women

★ Acquiring new skills fosters ongoing growth.

★ Building productive alliances is important.

★ "Mindercise" is as crucial to your well-being as physical exercise.

★ Overcome the barriers of fear and guilt to activate your positive power.

★ Advocacy for change requires positive power.

★ **The top ten positive power lessons are:**

1. I need to set limits and engage in adequate self-care.
2. I welcome mistakes as an indicator that I am pushing my limits and being all I can be.
3. I create security by developing my own competencies.
4. I seek the respect of others and recognize that some people will be uncomfortable around me.
5. I need to ask for what I want to reach my goals.
6. I need to be discriminating in my interactions with others.
7. I need to understand the rules and be flexible.
8. I need to engage in positive self-talk and monitor over-responsibility.
9. I want to make waves and be a change catalyst.
10. I acknowledge my accomplishments and seek appropriate recognition.

4

Women of Yesterday and Today

"…women are certainly not invisible any longer, nor are they any longer represented merely as victims."

—*Sandra Bem, Author, Researcher*

Why History
Is Important

New paths spring from history, and insights are learned from those who went before us. This chapter couples your understanding of socialization patterns and the development of positive power skills with historical and legislative insights. For women, the past provides the key to our future. Just as a psychologist must understand a patient's developmental history to provide proper patient care, an understanding of the past gives a contextual framework to design appropriate strategies for future change. Women need to incorporate historical perspectives to develop strategies for future advancement.

The history of the Women's Movement has had an impact on all our lives. The decade of your birth strongly influenced your perception of options. Many times women in their twenties and thirties seize personal options with a natural enthusiasm, but little awareness of the sacrifices of the women that have preceded them. Women in their forties and fifties straddle the traditional roles of their mothers and the new options they helped create. Awareness of female contributions is minimized by the erratic attention of the media and history books to women's achievements. Remember, it has been "his-story" more than "her-story" in the media.

Even intelligent, well-educated women often have a minimal knowledge of the number of exceptional women who have left their mark in science, literature, and social progress. Although women's studies programs continue to come under significant attack, these programs are to be applauded for the increased research and celebration of the many significant accomplishments of women. In the 1990's, these changing times allow women to learn of influential women who have led the way to new roles for women. Knowledge of the history of women in society allows women, as they enter the new millennium, to learn of the foundation for their increasing possibilities. The importance of history as a foundation for personal decision-making is reinforced in all schools of psychology. In particular, if a woman is to develop and use power, she needs to utilize prior role models of women who have used their power effectively and made a difference.

A lack of knowledge of history will limit a woman's awareness of her available tools for mobilizing change. The advantage of having a tool of historical knowledge was demonstrated to me graphically by an exchange with a psychology doctoral student. We attended a national convention for the Association for the Advancement of Behavior Therapy at which Betty Friedan was one of the featured speakers. The opportunity to meet the author of the *Feminine Mystique,* a book that provided a major catalyst for the Second Wave of feminism, was an exciting experience for me. I was trying to contain my excitement as I secured a front row seat when the bright, articulate, young, doctoral student leaned over and whispered "Who is Betty Friedan?" Even as I answered her, I knew immediately that this book delineating a new path for women must include feminist history—the past "waves" of the Women's Movement.

The First Wave of Feminism

The first ripples of feminism date back as far as 1792 with the publication of Mary Wollstonecraft's book *A Vindication of the Rights of Woman.* The recent 1996 reprinting reflects the still-contemporaneous nature of her writing. Mary Wollstonecraft was an outrageous woman in her time—she broke away from societal constraints to have an affair, a child out of wedlock, and then a marriage while pregnant a second time. Wollstonecraft writes poignantly of the struggle of women to obtain an education, and sharply portrays the difficulty of receiving an education in areas other than the "womanly" tasks of cooking and sewing. She graphically describes the frustration of a woman with an intellectual curiosity and passion for life forced to creatively maneuver to achieve an academic education. She lived in a time when educated women were often relegated to the role of tutor with semi-servant status. Defying the rigid rule that she should not demean her femininity by learning subjects of a "manly nature," Wollstonecraft learned all that she could and argued for equal educational opportunities for women. As a British writer, her writings reflect the international momentum for women's rights. Unfortunately, this remarkable woman died at the age of thirty-eight, shortly after giving birth to her second child, a girl who would become the author, Mary Wollstonecraft Shelley.

The fledgling feminist momentum continued after Wollstonecraft, and continued with varying momentum through 1963. During this period, there were active suffrage efforts and a political momentum grew to allow women to pursue education, address reproductive health issues, and secure voter franchise. In 1826, a public high school for girls opened in both Boston and New York and others followed. Once educational opportunities began to open a crack, momentum was gathered to open the door more widely.

In 1848, in the United States, the Women's Rights Convention was held in Seneca Falls, New York. This convention was attended by three hundred women, and was organized by the reformers Elizabeth Cady-Stanton and Lucretia Mott. The convention was a focus for strong, influential women of the age, and an outcome was the Declaration of Sentiments. These Sentiments declared that all women and men are equal, and called for legal, social, and political equality with men. The Sentiments demanded the right to vote, and the Women's Rights Convention launched the American campaign for women's suffrage. In 1851, less than five years after the Seneca Falls Convention, the Female Medical College of Pennsylvania was founded as the first women's college in the world. Women began to be trained as nurses in areas previously forbidden to them.

On March 8, 1857, hundreds of women garment workers in New York City staged a strike against low wages, long hours, and poor working conditions. This was one of the first organized labor actions by women in the world. Since 1975, this date has been immortalized by the United Nations as International Women's Day, and is the day selected for the publication of this book. International Women's Day symbolizes the activation of women's positive power to reshape society. Moreover, the labor of women must be celebrated with no artificial limits. We are an international community and the women's movement stretches beyond nationalistic boundaries.

As mentioned earlier, the Women's Movement first began as an international effort. During the First Wave, in 1878 an International Women's Rights Conference was held in France. In 1902, ten countries were represented at the International Women's Suffrage Conference in Washington, D.C., at which Susan B. Anthony presided. The political skills of women were further reflected in their formation of organizations. Two years later, the International Alliance of Women was formed. The international momentum of the First Wave continued throughout the first half of the century, and, in 1947, the United Nations Commission on the Status of Women was established.

It was not until 1920 that women were granted the right to vote across the nation, but it is interesting to note that many individual states granted the right for women to vote well before that time. The first state that granted women the right to vote was in Wyoming in 1890, the second was Colorado in 1893. Apparently, the western settlers of this country had a keen appreciation of the contributions of women. The First Wave of feminism not only achieved the right to vote, but in 1923 the Federal Civil Service voted for equal pay for equal work for all employees. The formation of the League of Women Voters, established in 1920, showed, once again, how the women of the First Wave recognized the importance of creating an organizational structure to encourage political gains.

The Women's Movement throughout time has been intertwined with issues of motherhood. Pregnancy, although a profound event in many women's lives, can also limit options. The image of keeping a woman "barefoot and pregnant" has been encouraged as a way to keep "women in line." Thus, birth control was also crucial to widening the opportunities for women. In 1916, Margaret Sanger, a public health nurse in New York City, opened the first family planning clinic in Brooklyn. Sanger crusaded for birth control options for women, providing a significant wedge in the door for women to expand possibilities in their lives.

Women's accomplishments continued to grow throughout the First Wave of feminism, a trend illustrated by Nobel Prize awards. Edith Wharton was the first woman to receive the Pulitzer Prize for fiction in 1921, and received an honorary degree from Yale University in 1923. Later, in 1931, Jane Addams was recognized as the first woman to win the Nobel Peace Prize for her work as a notable pacifist.

The years of the First Wave, spanning from 1792 through 1963 were tumultuous, and were affected by two world wars. As men in the thousands marched to protect the country, women were called upon to work the factories, the shops, and keep the "home fires" burning. When the Second World War was over, there was no turning back, and as the women achieved more and more varied experiences in their lives, the paths for women continued to widen and widen and widen.

The Second Wave of Feminism

Change always causes controversy, and expanding the opportunities of women and caused—is still causing—more controversy than any other social movement. Historical interpretations of the waves of the feminist movement are varied and often divergent. As a psychologist, not a historian, I mark the pivotal points of change by swells in our culture as reflected in books, legislation, and the language of everyday discussions. In 1963, feminist issues in both literature and legislation converged, creating a swell of movement that could not be ignored, and can be termed "The Second Wave."

President Kennedy had created a Commission on the Status of Women, which released a report in 1963. This same year Betty Friedan published the *Feminist Mystique*, and catapulted women into the Second Wave, also known as the Contemporary Women's Movement. Betty Friedan continued to widen the paths of options for women with a critical eye to evaluating the traditional roles of wife and mother. In this banner year, the U.S. Equal Pay Act was passed, and this law continued the momentum for equity and economic advancement.

Once again, organizations were created to focus the power being acquired by advances in women's rights. During the Second Wave, the National Organization for Women (NOW) was formed in 1966. In 1971, the National Women's Political Caucus was formed in Washington, D.C. During this period, women's organizations began to proliferate rapidly. Among the numerous organizations formed were: The National Women's Health Network, The Coalition of Labor Union Women, and The National Women's Study Association. By the mid-1990s, women organizations proliferated beyond accurate accounting. As the new millennium approaches, over six thousand organizations exist for equality of rights and opportunities for women.

Politically, women elected to Congress formed the Congressional Congress for Women's Issues (CCWI) in 1977 as a bipartisan organization with two co-chairs—one Democrat and one Republican. The Women's Research & Education Institute (WREI) was founded as the research and education arm of this caucus. Unfortunately, the status of the CCWI changed in 1994 when Congress abolished all legislative service organizations. However, WREI survives today as a non-profit organization dedicated to education and research on the status of women in society. The expansion of women's organizations reflected the pervasive activism of American women, and these organizations provided safe havens for women to hone their positive power skills.

The Second Wave of feminism was marked by "consciousness raising groups" fostering a recognition of female "sisterhood" with other women. The sisterhood component of the Second Wave created a powerful recognition of common desires, common threads, and the value of networking together. The battle cry of the "sisterhood" was the belief "*personal is political.*" Woman's struggles were examined in the context of the social and political climate. This slogan reflects that personal problems women encounter are connected to the political and social climate in which they live. The Second Wave of feminism brought to light that many women do not experience a great deal of pathology, rather that their problems in living are a reflection of an oppressive environment.

A problematic aspect of the "sisterhood" concept was the perception of women versus men. The unfortunate beginning of a gender war was a by-product of the female outcry for an expansion of life choices. Baby boomers remember clearly the excitement of women rallies; the heady feeling of Helen Reddy singing, *I am Woman, Hear Me Roar;* and the zeal with which women sought out women of like mind. The women of the Second Wave became the "instigators" for female leadership, whereas the "inheritors" will be the women of the Third Wave who have developed the capacity to utilize positive power and to generate a meaningful agenda.

A conflict was inherent in the activities of the Second Wave of feminism as a new awareness enlarged the path for women and vied for the traditional views of women's roles. Women were receiving mixed messages: get an education, be sure to find a good husband, find a good job, stay home and raise children—to highlight just a few. Many women then and now feel, at their core, that the worst fate is to be unmarried. More-over, breaking out of traditional female career roles in the 1960s and 1970s remained difficult. As an example, despite conscious-raising groups, many women first choose a "pink collar" job in education. A pink collar job is a job that is highly sanctioned and encouraged for women. An education job was encouraged as safe, and one which would allow women to be home with children. The message was women have limited options. For women with high grades, there was no structure within the college or within their family for considering, much less encouraging, a wider range of options.

During the Second Wave, legislation continued to proliferate. This legislation would begin to "turn the tide" and open doors of op-portunities that were previously closed. In 1972, Title IX of the Education Amendment was enacted and prohibited sex discrimina-tion in student admissions, employee hiring, and student athletics. The impact of this educational amendment was significant for women in opening formerly all male schools to women, and in expanding ath-letic opportunities. Title VII of the Civil Rights Act of 1964 made it unlawful for an employer to discriminate on the basis of sex, race, color, religion, or national origin. The Title VII provisions included all as-pects of employment such as hiring, training, promotion, firing, pay, benefits, and any other working condition. In 1978, Title VII was ex-tended even further to prohibit discrimination because of pregnancy or childbirth. In 1986, the Supreme Court included sexual harass-ment as a form of sexual discrimination prohibited under Title VII of the 1964 Civil Rights Act. Later, in 1991, the Civil Rights Act increased protection against sex discrimination by adding significant financial penalties, the ability to obtain punitive damages, and the ability to claim compensation for back pay and medical bills from employers. The Civil Rights laws are enforced by the Equal Employment Opportunity Com-mission (EEOC). Significant legislative gains, with additional legal teeth, were achieved in this Second Wave of feminism.

During this same time period, the Equal Rights Amendment (ERA) to the constitution, first proposed in 1923, was finally passed by Congress in 1972. However, constitutional law requires that the ERA be ratified by two-thirds of the States in the Union, and this ratification could not be achieved by the ten-year deadline of 1982. A backlash was building against feminism, and muddled messages caused the ERA to fail to be passed. The ERA was, in fact, quite simple, and would have added a statement to the U.S. Constitution: "Equality of rights under the law shall not be denied or abridged by the United States nor by any State on account of sex." It is a sad commentary that mixed messages of the meaning of equal rights began to swirl around during the Second Wave of feminism, and this contributed to the defeat of the ERA measure. Incipient backlash to the Women's Movement began to cause distortion of the feminist message, and the distortions were derived from varied sources.

The waves of the Women's Movement were described as waves of destruction for the family structure. Given the emotional appeal of children and family, the Women's Movement began to suffer from significant attacks, and the issues of equity began to be muddled with other issues. Susan Faludi, in her well-researched book *Backlash*, recounted case after case of a bias in reporting facts about women. She noted hundreds of stories where "negative news" that would discourage women were well-reported despite questionable sources. In contrast, well-researched reports showing the optimism for women were relegated to the back pages. Thus, an inaccurate image of women in distress, rather than women in power continued to emerge. Susan Faludi presented a frightening insight into orchestrated attempts to erode the gains of the Women's Movement. In a compelling four hundred and sixty pages, the hidden agendas of *Good Housekeeping* magazine to pharmaceutical companies were exposed.

Backlash's exposé reports that there has been media distortion of the status of women. Women continue to be portrayed as happiest in the home performing "womanly" tasks. Women's multiple roles of work, marriage, and motherhood are portrayed as endangering family life and creating "burn-out" for women. Thus, a media image emerges of over-whelmed women, yearning to be home full-time. This image does not accurately reflect the reality of the experiences of women or the results of multiple research studies. Life satisfaction research consistently reports full-time work combined with marriage and children enhances the lives of women and their families. Part of the media misperceptions may result from women being under-represented in the media. Women comprise only eight percent (8%) of newspaper management staff, less than twenty-five percent (25%) of television and radio news directors, and males continue to dominate guest interviews of radio and television. Even on the government-funded National Public Radio, eighty-five percent (85%) of the regular commentators are men. Unfortunately, the clarity and simplicity of equal rights and utilization of the talents of women and men became heavily clouded by these media distortions. This cloud hangs over the women's movement today.

Not only did the issues of equity in opportunity and economics become clouded as the backlash fed the controversy, but the Women's Movement began to splinter into many divisions. The message of feminism now has become more and more distorted. Betty Friedan, when she left the Presidency of the National Organization for Women in 1970, stated that sexual politics were already dividing women's strengths. Sandra Bem's fascinating book, *The Lenses of Gender: Transforming the Debate on Sexual Inequality*, includes a chronicling of the battles between feminist theorists that emerged during the Second Wave of feminist advocacy.

Although the message of equity becomes muddled, the international movement for equity continued to gain momentum. In 1979, the United Nations General Assembly adopted the Convention on the Elimination of All Forms of Discrimination Against Women. In the following year, the United Nations Second World Conference of Women was held in Copenhagen. Appropriately, the Second Wave saluted the First Wave of feminism in 1992, with the Women's Rights National Historical Park, which opened at the site of the first Women's Rights

Convention in Seneca Falls, New York. Symbolically, the "Mrs." title became only one of many salutation titles that women can have, and, in 1986, the *New York Times* accepted "Ms." as an appropriate title. The *New York Times* is viewed by many as a premiere barometer of American social changes, and is highly respected by corporate America. Therefore, the symbolism of 1986 reflects the different power position that women have achieved. Of course, humorists might note that in 1981 Sandra Day-O'Connor became the first woman to sit on the Supreme Court, but it took the *New York Times* until 1986 to acknowledge the title of "Ms."

During the Second Wave, divorce was no longer an exception in American society. Clearly, the earlier message of the importance of getting an Mrs. Degree as part of security planning in life was not an accurate message for countless women. Although having a spouse and having children can be significant sources of life satisfaction, they are not security blankets. At one period of my practice, over thirty percent (30%) of my practice was counseling women who had been married over twenty years and were now experiencing divorce. These women experienced intense anger. Many of the women had dropped out of college, devoted themselves to their husband's career, and felt abandoned and betrayed by their husbands. The women believed that if they were supportive and caring that the marriage would continue. Over eighty percent (80%) of these women had not been gainfully employed for more than fifteen years, viewed themselves as having few marketable skills, and were emotionally devastated.

In addition to the emotional devastation of divorce, each woman faced a significant reduction in economic lifestyle. In most cases, the women also lacked confidence in their ability to obtain gainful employment, and often believed no one would hire them. The secluded, protective environment of their marital homes had left these women fearful of presenting their talents for employment, and doubtful that the talents were useful in the business world. Despite their being household managers, having significant organizational skills, being well-versed in priority setting and management, these women had not received wages for their work. This lack caused them to devalue their own talents and expect that others would as well. Therapy, support groups, and community resources combined to educate newly divorced women on their considerable talents and facilitate their transition to independent lives.

Over the past years, hundreds of women have passed through my office, and I have been struck by their level of confusion. One of the special challenges for women with an increased number of options is the increased number of decisions, as well as the increased complexity of the decision-making process. Human psychology tends to make us sort information so that the information becomes more manageable, but often the sorting process can lead to oversimplification. For example, quickly sorting information can make us to fall into the trap of polarity thinking of experiencing either "all-or-nothing" or "either-or," and not perceiving a continuum of options. An example is Amy, an ambitious woman who has had significant career success in her thirties, but who came into my office distraught by her emotional tugs to have children. She had difficulty sleeping, and could not walk through the mall—seeing babies—without dissolving into tears. Amy's thinking was in the either-or pattern, and she saw her difficulty as either career or children, with nothing in between.

This either-or thinking is very common, both throughout history and in individual psychological development. In actuality, study after psychological study demonstrates that the most satisfied women are those who combine career with children and marriage. Many of my patients entered my office struggling with what they perceived as a necessary fork in their life, and left with a recognition of the ability to integrate multiple roles, rather than abandoning one to acquire another. Amy was able to adjust her thinking and decrease her turmoil. She became less conflicted and open to integrating career and family.

Integrating roles was a significant contribution of the Second Wave of feminism, which dispelled the myth that "women can't have it all!" The majority of present-day working women are "doing it all" and doing it well. Several psychological and business studies have shown that the happiest women are working, married, and have children. Further, many of these women are in management positions, just below the Glass Ceiling. A *New York Times* article by Jane E. Brody discussed the need to dispel the stereotype that marriage and children are a barrier to career advancement. As Jane Brody stated, "In this country, the working mother of young children is no longer the exception. She is now the rule."

Thus, the Second Wave of feminism dramatically increased the different life options that women could consider. No longer were there occupations or athletics or places that women could not go alone, or with other women. Women were no longer viewed as needing chaperones, necessitating male companionship, or primarily as breeders for future generations. During the Second Wave of feminism, women were able to break constraints and travel the world both literally and symbolically with an ocean of options. However, the multiplicity of options also caused confusion, mixed messages, and launched a gender war. Women and men were often pitted against each other as adversaries, rather than as having complimentary qualities. Additionally, feminism was becoming viewed as anti-male, anti-family, and as a hostile force in the society. Many women embraced the principals of feminism, but were very hesitant to describe themselves as a feminist. Thus the Second Wave needed to end, and the Third Wave needed to arrive.

The Third Wave of Feminism

The Third Wave of feminism is still a ripple, which began in the 1990s and hopefully will reach a tidal wave crescendo early in the new millennium. The Third Wave reflects a shift away from past categorizations of abilities, to focus on women's strengths while recognizing gender differences. Mutual gender respect, and acknowledging the talents of both women and men, is necessary for success in the new global economy. Women of the nineties are beginning to stride toward the new millennium with a beginning sense of their own power. In 1992, the number of women in Congress doubled and was termed "the year of the woman" in politics. The essential tools that women will need in the Third Wave of feminism involve overcoming fears of power and embracing power with wisdom. The ability of women to embrace positive power and use it effectively will be a catalyst for changing cultural norms nationally and internationally.

The arrival of the Third Wave was confirmed by the creation of the Third Wave Foundation, a national activist philanthropic organization for young women between the ages of fifteen and thirty. Rebecca Walker, Dawn Martin, Amy Richards, and Kathryn Gund founded the organization with the goal of creating a supportive community, a source where women could be encouraged to take control of their lives before external forces control them. The Third Wave Foundation exemplifies the emphasis on the usage of positive power and creating a spectrum of choices. The ongoing evolution in feminist thinking is strikingly portrayed in the book *to be real: Telling the Truth and Changing the Face of Feminism*, edited by Rebecca Walker. This book portrays the necessity for welcoming diversity and allowing voices with varying opinions to reflect the multifaceted dimensions of women. Hopefully, the Third Wave of feminism will focus on diversity, include all ages, and emphasize a societal formation that will offer both men and women powers of unlimited choices and move beyond past gender wars.

The beginning movements of the Third Wave are reflected in the 1990 U.S. Act for Better Childcare, and the 1993 U.S. Family and Medical Leave Act. Both laws reflect the acceptance of women in the workforce as a norm and the need to give attention to creating societal support for both women and men to cope with family and work demands. The international movement continues, with the 1993 United Nations Conference on Human Rights Proclamation that any violence against women is a human rights violation. Moreover, the United Nations Fourth World Conference of Women was held in Beijing, China, in 1995.

In July of 1998, the delegates of the National Organization for Women gathered to celebrate one hundred and fifty years of the

Women's Rights Movement. At that time, a 1998 Declaration of Sentiments of the National Organization for Women was issued. This Declaration of Sentiments is a reflection of ongoing momentum from the initial Declaration of Sentiments that was declared in 1848 at the first Women's Rights Convention in Seneca Falls, New York. An excerpt from the 1998 Declaration of Sentiments reflects the ongoing momentum of feminism and the embracing of multiple diverse viewpoints:

"We bring passion, anger, hope, love and perseverance to create this vision for the future:

We envision a world where women's equality and women's empowerment to determine our own destinies is a reality;

We envision a world where women have equal representation in all decision-making structures of our societies;

We envision a world where social and economic justice exist, where all people have the food, housing, clothing, health care, and education they need;

We envision a world where there is recognition and respect for each person's intrinsic worth as well as the rich diversity of the various groups among us;

We envision a world where non-violence is the established order;

We envision a world where patriarchal culture and male dominance no longer oppress us or our earth;

We envision a world where women and girls are heard, valued, and respected.

Our movement, encompassing many issues and many strategies, directs our love for humanity into action that spans the world and unites women.

Clearly, feminism is a continuing proactive movement for social change. The ongoing momentum for feminists' goals is further reflected in the National Women's Equality Act for the Twenty-First Century. The National Women's Equality Act was sponsored by the National Council of

Women's Organizations, a bipartisan network of leaders from over one hundred organizations representing more than six million women. The principals for the future clearly have been elucidated. The challenge for the Third Wave of feminism is to have the principals translated into legislative and societal reality through actions of both women and men.

The international arena for advancing feminism remains focused on lobbying in the United States for ratification of the United Nations Treaty, the Convention on the Elimination of All Forms of Discrimination Against Women (CEDAW). The United States is the only industrialized democracy that has not ratified this treaty. Nationally, the National Organization for Women's campaign is mobilizing to elect two thousand feminist candidates by the new millennium. Women comprise over half the United States' population, yet comprise less than fifteen percent (15%) of Congress. Clearly, political activism needs to gain more momentum.

Organizations advocating for equalization of rights are many. Equal Rights Advocates (ERA) is a diverse legal organization that has been an effective voice protecting the rights of women. The ERA is a San Francisco-based legal center who has defended several cases enforcing the teeth of these legislative acts. Additionally, ERA is a resource center for the legal rights of women.

As feminism moves forward, Jean Baker-Miller raised the issues of enacting the principles of the Third Wave in *Toward A New Psychology Of Women*. She asks: "How do we conceive a society organized so that it permits both the development and mutuality of all people? How do we get there? How do women move from a powerless empty valued position to fully valued effectiveness? How do we get the power to do this, even if we do not want or need power to control or submerge others?" These questions remain to be answered, but answers derived from the Third Wave of feminism will articulate gender differences rather than gender inequality, and facilitate the utilization of positive power to achieve mutually agreed upon societal goals. The future of the new millennium requires a collaboration of women and men with an appreciation of gender differences.

The Glass Ceiling

As mentioned earlier, a hindrance to the Third Wave of feminism and the gender collaboration of women and men is the Glass Ceiling. The limiting barrier of the Glass Ceiling prevents qualified women and minorities from advancing upward into top level management positions where they can be more effective in promoting change. The Glass Ceiling describes the frustrating experience of having your career path halted by unknown factors.

The U.S. Department of Labor's Glass Ceiling Commission's final report was issued in 1995, titled, *A Solid Investment: Making Full Use of the Nation's Human Capital.* Observations from this commission and other researchers indicate that the Glass Ceiling stems from androcentrism, or viewing male behaviors as the norm. Organizational and psychological research found that people tend to promote people like themselves. Therefore, the predominance of white males in top executive positions tends to perpetuate white males in upper leadership positions. Lynn Morley-Martin, former U.S. Secretary of Labor and Illinois Congresswoman, stated, "The Glass Ceiling hinders not only the individuals but society as a whole. It effectively cuts our pool of potential corporate leaders by half. It deprives our economy of new leaders, new sources of creativity—the 'would be' pioneers of the business world."

The Glass Ceiling is a concern addressed by many. The Chicago Area Partnership was formed in a response to the Glass Ceiling, which was viewed as a barrier to economic growth. The Partnership was formed in 1992 from a combination of community and government representatives gathered to discuss workplace issues. The Chicago Area Partnership report noted, "The criteria used to identify . . . high potentials are based on tradition and perceived 'comfort factors' which tend to favor white men. Individual managers, frequently white males, 'groom' their own successors, perpetuating the concentration of white males in higher positions."

The Glass Ceiling is contrary to the concept of equal opportunity for equal talent, a concept woven into American society. The Glass Ceiling is not only an economic issue for the new global economy in terms of the bottom line for corporations, but also places an artificial lid on a large portion of the talent pool. Several legislative measures have addressed this issue. In addition to Title VII of the Civil Rights Act of 1964, Executive Order 11246 also prohibited discrimination in hiring women on the basis of race, color, religion, sex, and national origin. Further, the Age Discrimination Employee Act, the Pregnancy Discrimination Act, the American Disabilities Act, and the Civil Rights Act of 1991 establish protections. However, even in government service there remains a significant disparity in the proportion of women versus men filling management grade levels thirteen through fifteen.

The recommendations of the Federal Glass Ceiling Commission Final Report noted that the Glass Ceiling must be removed if the United States is to utilize all available talent. Only if the Glass Ceiling is abolished can the insights and talents of all working people be utilized to their fullest potential. The presence of the Glass Ceiling denies millions of Americans the opportunity for both economic and personal advancement. By the new millennium, two-thirds of the new labor force entrants will be minorities and women moving toward the Glass Ceiling. For this and other reasons, it is important to move minorities and women through this artificial barrier into upper management positions, not only for the utilization of their talents, but also for their insight and abilities to tap into many segments of the consumer market.

An interesting contrast exists between the findings of this commission and the backlash phenomena in American society against affirmative action. As the commission noted in its report, affirmative action is greatly misunderstood. Affirmative action is not the quota system as often misdescribed, but rather is a system that casts a wider net than is presently available to train recruits and promote advancement for women and other minorities. The Glass Ceiling barrier effects two-thirds of the population and creates a significant economic toll on American businesses. Affirmative action programs develop career pathways to move beyond the Glass Ceiling barriers. You cannot travel a road that is not present.

The *Journal of Applied Psychology* noted that disparities between women's and men's salary levels and promotions exist even though women had accomplished all the "right stuff" with their education, their positions within a company, and accepting transfers. The Glass Ceiling has been well-documented as a subtle, limiting life factor for women and other minorities. Women are now challenged to move beyond the wall of tradition and stereotypes separating them from top executive levels. Both women and the corporation are the losers, as long as the Glass Ceiling remains.

A study from the Center for Creative Leadership stated, "We face a critical time for female executives in corporate America. Women have struggled to get into management, and some companies have also struggled to get them there. They have made significant headway in moving up the corporate ladder, only to be stopped dead at the top." The mindset of being "stopped dead" is troubling for both the United States society and for women and minorities. The challenge for the new millennium is for women and minorities to strategically activate their positive power in new ways to remove the Glass Ceiling from American society. With only a small portion of this century remaining, women are positioning now to move beyond the Glass Ceiling in the twenty-first century. Your utilization of your positive power skills will be the key to leadership positions, moving the Glass Ceiling to the status of past history, and shaping society in new directions for the new millennium.

Star Points

★ Before you can create a new path, you need to know where you have been.

★ Education and data are important tools in maximizing your life experience.

★ The First Wave of Feminism promoted education and the vote for women both nationally and internationally.

★ The Second Wave of Feminism widened the "opportunity path," legislated equity in the United States, promoted equity internationally, and left multiple mixed messages in the United States culture.

★ The Third Wave of Feminism is activating for the new millennium. The Third Wave of Feminism will reflect the information age, the global economy, appreciation of gender differences, and gender collaboration.

★ The Glass Ceiling is an artificial barrier that limits access to the talents of women and inhibits the profitability of businesses and political vision.

★ Feminism has been a misunderstood movement that has received significant societal backlash.

★ Women activating their positive power skills will catapult to leadership positions in the new millennium, move beyond the Glass Ceiling, and be change agents for society.

5

Feminism
Needs
a Facelift

*"Feminism lacks positive imagery, even
something as basic as a widely understood,
positive logo."*

—*Naomi Wolf, Author*

Distortions-
Distortions

I have experienced many highlights in my life as a long-time card-carrying member of the National Organization for Women; I experienced the consciousness-raising groups, struggles to not be patronized, and pride in meeting fascinating, intelligent women at NOW meetings. For me, feminism is a proud badge. Presently, memories of my own experiences, recollections of patients, and the results of months of research flash through my mind with conflicting images. While I have spent more than a decade sequestered in my office working with patients, the amount of divisiveness and distortion on the meaning of feminism has multiplied in the world. Feminism, in many people's eyes, has truly taken on a new perception as a "capital F" word. *Time* magazine's, June 29, 1998, cover article raised the issue "Is Feminism Dead?" This article reflected the distortions and problematic image of feminism today. Accurate and positive information on the feminist movement is not widely disseminated. Feminists have contributed to their own image difficulties by a failure to embrace different perspectives, and attacking other feminists for differing ideological positions.

Divisiveness serves no positive purpose. Divisiveness drains the energies of the women's movement and paints women as a caricature. Women are individuals with different beliefs, different viewpoints, and a spectrum of perspectives, all of which are dazzling with diversity and richness. Feminists, be they female or male, have one issue to focus on—freedom to choose options with no artificial barriers. The heart of feminism goes beyond gender.

The heart of feminism is equal opportunity for all. The richness of your life is increased by the collaboration of women and men and the celebration of the talents of both genders. Women are not secondary citizens and their talents can no longer be minimized. Women want to foster equal rights, equal opportunities, equal responsibilities, and equal respect. How these expanded opportunities will be activated is each individual's choice.

To maintain the core focus of creating a spectrum of choices for both sexes, anger and adversarial positions have to be jettisoned. Anger is a draining emotion. Anger triggers a physiological response in your body that depresses your immune system and makes you vulnerable to a disease process. Anger drains you of energy, of reason. Women have to release their anger and activate their positive power. Although it is true that many women have been victimized, remaining a victim mires you in the past. Victimization does not have to be a life sentence. Given appropriate recognition and utilization of positive power, feminists—both women and men—can reshape society, both nationally and internationally.

The different faces of feminism have a common core theme. All types of feminism involve activating the talents of women. The path that will best utilize the talents of women is the source of controversy. However, create multiple paths and allow each woman and each man choose their own path. The movement needs to focus on numerous paths, not divisive ongoing debates for finding the "right" path.

In life there are multiple rights, for life does not exist in a neat package with clear rights and wrongs. Each situation and each individual needs to design their own life map. The key is to have varied paths open and available. Regrettably, the presence of the Glass Ceiling may stop your path prematurely and unnecessarily, to everyone's detriment.

I call on all feminists—female and male, whether you are a capital feminist, a classical liberal feminist, a conservative feminist, a contemporary feminist, a cultural feminist, a diversity feminist, an equity feminist, an existential feminist, a general feminist, a liberal feminist, a missionary feminist, a modern feminist, an orthodox feminist, a power feminist, a radical feminist, a socialist feminist, a victim feminist, a feminist by any title—to remember the common theme. Feminism does not have to be a polluted word. Women shy away from feminism as labeling them as militant, and dictating a specific ideology that must be followed as a blueprint of life. This viewpoint must be altered. We need to eliminate in-fighting and focus on a common theme of *all options open for everyone.*

The distortions of the feminist movement are distracting us from the personal and political actions needed. Many feminist writers are shouting this message from the rooftops. The insightful book *Women, Sex and Power in the Nineties,* states "We feel a similar urgency today, as we watch the feminist enterprise that has transformed our lives being distorted, commodified and/or vilified . . . ." Distortions and misinformation are multiplying daily. In your words and actions, you need to dispel the myths. Moving beyond the Glass Ceiling requires a respect for women and reeducation on the talents and abilities of women.

Anti-Male

A major distortion is the belief that, if one is a feminist, one is against men. For years, society has engaged in a hostility to women, *misogyny.* Feminists do not want to mimic this adversarial behavior with hostility to men, *misandrism.* The belief system of feminists as anti-male stems from the discomfort that many men experience when they are challenged and held accountable. Prior to technological advances, the structure of society created a delineation of roles for men and women that was structured with divisions of labor with women's talents under-utilized. In recent history, men have held the majority of decision-making positions in both government and the corporate world. As the divisions of labor have eroded in the last century, gender no longer dictates life labors. Women and men vie for the tasks of life. However, the ambiguity involved with these changes, creates confusion and fear. As women have lobbied the male decision-makers and been forceful, the discomfort with this advocacy has fueled a misperception that feminists dislike men.

Women have husbands and sons which they treasure and love. Women recognize that male companionship can add richness to life. Male companionship, although not a life necessity, can be a life-enhancing experience. For the future of civilization, women and men need to work together, not only for propagation, but in an effective collaboration, celebrating differences and respecting each other. Advocating female positive power is not seeking to decrease male power.

Power, like love, is not a finite concept. Love and positive power are umbrella terms that contain many raindrops of meaning. Love and power have similarities. The more love you give, the more positive energy and the more loving energy is created. The more positive power that you utilize the more that can be accomplished. Love and power are both activating forces. You do not have to put ourself on a love or power diet; you need to indulge yourself with as much love and power as you can. Positive power and love are to be shared and exchanged between the genders. You need to increase the amount of powerful and loving behaviors you express.

The extreme distortion of the belief that all feminists are anti-male is the image of feminism as controlled by lesbians. Lesbianism is a preference for women. Just as some women prefer to be with women, some men prefer to be with men. Your sexual orientation is a private matter that does not reflect your politics. Feminists do not fit into a neat descriptive category. The lesbian distortion creates discomfort for many heterosexual women who benefit greatly from the ability to network with other women.

A women's sexual opinion on men is not her feminist ideology. The anti-male agenda that has become so intertwined with feminism needs to be unraveled. Until this belief is unraveled, it chokes feminism and limits its ability to be effective.

As discussed repeatedly in this book, a tendency exists to engage in simplistic thinking, over-generalization, and black-and-white thinking to create polarities. Human behaviors do not operate on polarities, but rather our behaviors operate on a continuum. Successful, executive women have been mentored by women and men alike. The majority of successful executive women are married and with children. Women, as they pursue their corporate careers, are not engaged in a gender war. The focus of a woman's concern is complex. Women's rights are a part of a much larger political and economic story. In no way should feminism be construed as a campaign waged against men.

Men are not the enemy—feminist leaders such as Betty Freidan and numerous others have been saying this mantra for years, and I cannot emphasize it enough. The distortion of feminism as being anti-male stemmed from women's increased advocacy for their own rights, their own property, their own choices, and their needs to be treated equitably. Since men were often in the positions of power and held the key to the change in women's rights, they were lobbied for the changes. Female advocacy through negotiations with male power-brokers is not anti-male behavior, but is challenging the current power-brokers. In the future, both women and men will be approaching female and male power-brokers as they reach for their personal advancement.

It goes without saying that women have needed men, and men have needed women, over the millennia of human existence. Much of this need is rooted in our sensuality. Women and men enjoy their sensuality as an intricate part of our quality of life. Your sensuousness, your ability to have orgasm, and the incredible power of human touch have been amply demonstrated by research in human behavior between the opposite sex as well as the same sex. Touching and sensuousness add meaning and dimension to life.

Of course, perpetuating the species and allowing society to survive or civilization to continue requires the heterosexual sexual interaction necessary for propagation. For those women electing to birth a child, the experience is indescribable. The birth of my son is vividly etched in my mind with a sense of awe and profound joy. Women, both as the bearers of female and male offspring and as wives, cherish the men in their lives. Feminism does not contradict womanhood.

The Dangers of Gender Wars

The perception of a gender war between women and men continues the patriarchal momentum of adversarial interactions. For centuries, adversarial thinking has pitted individual against individual, corporation against corporation, and nation against nation. The realities of the new millennium dictate a new mindset. The new millennium brings a global economy with creative cooperation between nations and corporations. With the coming changes, women and men need to mirror the cooperative spirit required for the next century. Both women and men need to increase their understanding of gender differences to facilitate effective, cooperative behaviors. When either a female or a male makes assumptions based on gender rather than a rationale assessment of behaviors, significant dangers exist for misinterpretations, perceptions of victimization, and creations of power drains on your abilities.

Women and men need to interact as equally powerful talents who bring different perspectives to management and leadership. As collaborative exchanges increase, creative problem-solving will enhance the quality of life for all in the new millennium. The changing fabric of world society necessitates utilization of the talents of all individuals to cope with societal issues. Together, men and women, improve life quality both for themselves and for the world.

Ginger's Story

This clinical case is a prime example of jumping to conclusions rather than a careful assessment of facts. Without executive coaching, the female manager in the following discussion may have artificially short-circuited her career growth. Ginger was a married, thirty-one-year-old female manager of a pharmaceutical sales company. Ginger, prior to her sales position, had worked as a nurse. She was promoted to manager after being the lead salesperson in her office for three years. Prior to assuming the manager role, Ginger had been managed by a female manager. Once promoted to manager, she reported to a male regional manager, Bill. During Ginger's initial session, she alternated between short responses to answers with clenched teeth to verbose explanations of her behavior. Ginger stated, "I refuse to be treated this way . . . who does he think he is . . . I am so angry I can't talk." During treatment sessions, Ginger carefully examined the content of the requests that were made by the regional manager. As the sessions progressed, it became evident that more than eighty percent (80%) of the requests were appropriate work requests.

Her manager was a detailed individual who placed high demands for reports on all of his area managers. Bill's style of numerous written reports was in sharp contrast to Ginger's prior female manager who requested minimal paperwork. Additionally, Ginger had not factored into her perceptions the changing job tasks required for a manager's role. Her administrative functions were very different. Ginger was able to recognize that she had made assumptions that she was being treated differentially because of her sex, rather than taking into consideration Bill's management style and the requirements of her new position. Jumping to the conclusion that Bill was biased against women was a limiting approach. Managerial style, managerial behaviors, and the demands of your position need to be evaluated independently of gender assumptions.

Ginger was able to admit that her years as a nurse had created a backlog of resentment from treatment by some male doctors who thought M.D. stood for "Magnificent Deity." Ginger felt that her contributions, as part of the medical team, were often not adequately appreciated. Her past experiences were spilling into the present. Ginger was in danger of limiting her opportunities in the corporate world by using a "gender filter" to assess her interactions with her male manager.

At the end of therapy, Ginger was adjusting to the new demands of her position and found a significant decrease in her job stress. Ginger realized that it was in her best interest to have an open mind to the developing relationship between herself and her new supervisor. Clearly, her present interactions with her male supervisor were different from her prior interactions with her female supervisor. During sessions, I acquainted her with the work of Deborah Tannen, a psycholinguistic expert who developed the concept of "genderlects." Female and male communication patterns have many variances. As we reviewed gender differences in communication patterns, Ginger was able to be less offended by her manager—by Bill's directness and need to have the last word. As therapy progressed, Ginger was able to not personalize his comments and react with more comfort. Gender differences in communication and value systems need to be understood to facilitate women and men developing effective work teams.

Jim's Story

Women and men, when battling each other, waste their energy. When women and men become partners and address problems together, the problems can be surmounted easily. The next clinical example illustrates the dangers of gender assumptions from a male perspective. Jim, a forty-six-year-old divorced, male, was referred to my office by the corporate employee assistance program. Jim was vice president for a financial firm. He was being considered for promotion to executive vice president. The referral stated that Jim's promotion was being delayed due to his difficulty in managing a regional female manager, Susan. He came to the office agitated, annoyed, and defensive. His first statement was, "Am I here to get a lecture?"

Jim and I discussed his feelings about working with a female psychologist and issues that he had in working with women. Jim verbalized that his family stressed the importance of male pride, and the female manager that he was supervising was direct and persistent in her requests. During sessions, Jim struggled with the concept of interacting in a business environment with women who presented powerful behavior patterns. Jim was locked into the mindset of women being low keyed and accommodating in their demeanor. Stereotypes of gender exist in all of us. The important focus in the therapy was to recognize the stereotypic expectations and, once recognized, be able to counter his reactions. When Jim ended therapy, he still strongly believed that accommodating women were more feminine. On a personal level, he enjoyed quiet and demure women. On the other hand, Jim also recognized that he needed to monitor his stereotypic expectations and be respectful of a wider spectrum of behaviors from his female regional manager. Mutual respect and the right to have different opinions were the keys to unlocking Jim's difficulty with Susan.

Jim requested an appointment four months after the end of his coaching sessions. His attitude and demeanor in this session were dramatically different. Jim and I engaged in some good-natured bantering, as he handed me his new business card noting his promotion to executive vice president. During the session, Jim discussed his post-coaching changes which helped him open the options for both himself and all of his managers. Jim commented, "I never considered that gender stereotypes were a limiting factor in my life. I just never stopped to think in those terms. I appreciate the opportunity I had to readjust my thinking patterns." At the end of the session, he teasingly commented that he also wanted to update me on a new aspect of his personal life. Jim announced that he was engaged to be married and he laughingly referred to himself as a "new 90's man."

Anti-Beauty

The distortion that feminists are anti-beauty began with women allowing themselves to be more natural in appearance. The beauty industry is a large industry, which uses considerable visual advertising. Some of the public presentations of female images have caused many women to damage their bodies with eating disorders and unnecessary plastic surgery. Many women rejected these advertising pressures which tended to portray women as beautiful objects. Women do not want to be viewed as a body first and a person second. Women, as they began to increase their life options, wanted to be viewed not only for their "eye appeal," but also for their talents and abilities. As a result, many women elected to choose comfortable clothing, and a wider variety of wearing apparel choices became available to women.

Leaving the corsets and paraphernalia of past clothing styles behind, many women chose attire to reflect their job needs. Women who work in factories dress similarly to their male counterparts. Similarly, women in offices wear business-like attire. The choice was for clothing that suited the women's work role, and was not selected to set aside attractiveness.

The desire to be personally attractive still remains for both women and men. Even the word "attractive" conveys its intent—to draw attention, to collect gazes, to *attract.* Everyone enjoys admiring glances, getting compliments, and likes the feeling of "looking good." The criteria for "looking good," however, is a wide continuum of choices and styles. Once again, the danger is creating a black-and-white thinking between the beliefs that one must be dumpy to dress comfortably or one is only attractive when squeezing into a spandex dress and having breast implants. A large range of behavior exists between greasy hair, sloppy clothes, and the spandex special. Both women and men can retain their feminist ideology and still present themselves in an attractive manner.

Veronica Webb, a stunning model and the first African-American woman to sign a major cosmetic contract, wrote a fascinating chapter, in *to be real,* titled "How does a supermodel do feminism?". This entertaining chapter demonstrates that capitalizing on one's talents, whatever they may be, is a prudent choice in life. Veronica reflects the theme of this book: "The bottom line is how you do or don't use your power." Women who advocate for expanded options and equal respect come in all shapes and sizes, and possess a variety of looks. You can present yourself in your own unique style of beauty and still be an advocate for unlimited life options.

Anti-Family

The hue and cry across the land is that feminism and the women's movement will destroy the fabric of family life. This has been a fascinating distortion that has no basis in fact. What concerns me greatly is that this distortion in particular has negatively impacted the psychological health of women. Many women who work and contribute close to fifty percent (50%) of needed family income are racked with guilt that their working causes difficulties for their family. The working woman myth has been touted in the media for my entire lifetime.

Dispel this myth with a look at the research. The Center for Research on Women at Wellesley College in Massachusetts is a highly respected research facility. A fascinating monograph is *Research on the Effects of Women's Outside Employment: A Review for Clinical Practitioners.* This working paper was presented by Dr. Rosalind Barnett and reported a study of pediatricians. Study results found no differences between the children of employed and unemployed mothers in the risk of their children for problems behaviorally or medically. Over fifty years of research concludes that mothers' working status does not make a difference in child development. If anything, data appear to be accumulating that working mothers have a *positive* effect on children. Children of working mothers have a less gender stereotypic view of the world, are able to adjust to change more readily, and assume responsibility within the household which fosters increased self-esteem for children.

Additionally, the myth of job strain and negative spillover from job to home is just the opposite. Dr. Barnett reported in another study that, rather than a negative spillover from job to home, a positive spillover exists from job to home. The higher psychological health is among working women who have full-time jobs. An interesting research fact is that women who work part-time are in more danger of a negative spillover: economic constraints are higher, less resources for psychological reinforcement are present, and less esteem is available in their work environment. Another myth that needs to be dispelled is that women with children will be less effective on their jobs. Research has clearly demonstrated that women's job behaviors and women's home behaviors are independent. Numerous women in my clinical practice report a routine separation of work and family. Women, especially with their increased ability to multi-track and compartmentalize, are capable of separating their home and work responsibilities.

Healthy living is promoted by having multiple roles and multiple access to resources. The more mastery that you experience in your life, the more you can nurture and care for others. Research clearly documents the contributions of working women to family life. Working women add to family life emotionally and financially.

Neuter

The feminist movement mobilized to dispel limiting stereotypes of women and expand their behavioral repertoire. Gender-neutral terminology replaced weighted words that were reinforcing limitations on women. These and other gender-neutral actions gave rise to a concept of unisex. At times, the concept leans toward neuter (neither female and male) and at times toward androgyny (combined female and male), but the basis is a description of human behavior that is neither female and male. The term androgyny emerged as a common term in the psychological literature in the seventies. The androgynous term was defined as a balance of feminine and masculine behaviors. Unfortunately, the attempt to expand the behavioral repertoire of both women and men minimizes gender differences. Not only were gender differences minimized, the distortion that feminism neutered human beings became a negative perception.

At the beginning of the Second Wave, also known as contemporary feminism, women were rebelling against being viewed as the inferior sex, the second sex, the deficient sex, and the "less than" sex. As women advocated for parity, the emphasis was placed on ability to develop talents, equal intellectual potential, and equal ability to speak-up and speak-out, among other behaviors. The focus was on women moving from an inferior position to a position of equalized power with men.

However, the androgynous perspective became distorted to a belief that feminism meant that women and men were alike in all dimensions. This myth further expands the erroneous belief that, feminists, want to create a unisex society. Such a perception would ignore the fascinating differences between women and men. Once again, the myths and distortion do not reflect research. As will be discussed in more detail in the next chapter, women have unique ways of knowing. Women and men have differences in their language patterns, differences in the way they access information, differences in their competitive patterns, and differences in their emphasis on relationships. The list of the differences between women and men is extensive.

Not only are the differences extensive, no normal woman or normal man exists in real life. Normality is a statistical abstraction that does not exist. In reality, everyone is abnormal. You deviate from a mythical statistical average and have a unique combination of behaviors. Although recent research has demonstrated gender differences, the gender differences are activated along a continuum. This activation creates individual uniqueness. Human beings cannot be pigeonholed. In our complex world, you cannot afford to possess simplistic definitions of women and men.

Gender differences need to be continually researched, understood by both genders, and cross-training needs to be part of your life training. *Science* magazine discussed that women engineers who received "gender bending training" created different options for themselves. In particular, as you move into the new millennium with a global economy, men will benefit greatly from women's ease with language and ability to create information webs to rapidly process information. Similarly, women will benefit from cross-training by men to be more resilient to change, to focus less on worry behaviors, and engage in more consistent self-care. These are but a few examples of the ways that some women and some men may benefit from cross-gender training. Women and men need to celebrate and enjoy each other and to learn from each other. It is through collaborating on many levels that you will be able to focus on shaping a more tolerable world.

Women's Studies

Women's studies programs have come under multiple attacks over the years. The question is often raised, why have a women's studies program? Why not have a men's studies program? The reality of the last hundreds of years is that the majority of studies have been male studies. Whether it be psychological studies or medical studies, the majority of studies were conducted by men with male subjects. Thus, much of what we know about human functioning has used the male model. Clearly, the male model is not the only model of effective life functioning. Role models of achieving women need to be presented to girls and young women.

Women's studies programs perform important functions, particularly in developing a base of history and knowledge to identify diverse role models. In *Beyond Power*, Marilyn French stated, "Already, in only two decades, a huge body of feminist scholarship has been built. There is solid, brilliant, unimpeachable work by feminist historians, anthropologists and ethnologists, psychologists, ecologists, and sociologists. There is a small, endangered body of law decreeing equality that can stand as foundation for future action. There is feminist art, not enough perhaps to be called a tradition, but the start of one. Feminist ideas and values have permeated women's writing for over a century, constituting a history if not a tradition."

Women's studies programs have dramatically increased the knowledge base of women and how they function. Additionally, scholars who have had access to women's studies research have been mobilized to advocate for more attention to women's health problems. Women's studies courses also created a fertile environment for women to develop the power of their minds. Often in women studies classes, a collaborative and egalitarian spirit emerges that allows women to challenge their minds with more freedom and less concern with reprisal.

Women's studies programs have made major inroads in helping the voices of women be heard and elucidating the many ways that one can both learn and teach others. Once again, the emphasis is not that a women's way of knowing is superior to the men's way of knowing, but rather the emphasis is recognizing that differences exist and appreciating that the differences are to be celebrated and understood. Women's studies are bringing to light dimensions of human potential that have not been fully recognized or adequately valued. Also, women's studies classes are a valuable vehicle to teach positive power tools. Hats off to the women of courage who raised their voices to be heard throughout society! The commitment of women to further the understanding of women, to balance research and history, and to end oppression is to be applauded. Women's studies does not limit perspectives, it expands perspectives. The diversity and multiplicity of viewpoints, the impact of race as well as gender, social class, and the impact of ethnic background as well as gender creates a diversity well-suited to the global economy. Respect for all aspects of diversity is to be fostered.

Sisterhood

For me personally, sisterhood and feminism are meshed. I have yet to attend a meeting of The Association of Women in Psychology, a meeting of Division 35 of the American Psychological Association, a meeting of the National Organization for Women, a meeting of the Boston Women's Group, a meeting of the Women of Wisdom Power Breakfast Group, or a clinical staff meeting at the Center of Psychological Effectiveness without being profoundly impacted. The talents of other women and the gracious support that I have received from other women create an energy that continues to inspire and enrich my life. Although I have received support from men and this support continues in many areas of my life, the connectedness with other women speaks to my soul in a way that is difficult to articulate. Feminism is a political movement; feminism is not a particular ideology. Feminism promotes sisterhood. Feminism needs a new logo, a new media facelift, but it must not die. Only through feminist connections, whatever form they may take, are multiple opportunities for sisterhood experiences presented.

Women join together promoting each other's talents, seeking equitable treatment, and deploring all types of oppression. The magic of sisterhood can light up any room. The tragedy of present day feminism is that divisiveness is causing many women to avoid feminist opportunities to connect in sisterhood. A major marketing and public relations effort is needed to create a renewed unity. The backlash effect must be reduced, distortions dispelled and new synergy created between women and men— only in this way can we the ongoing power of sisterhood be guaranteed.

Sisterhood needs to emerge into the mainstream. This networking isn't a heavy ponderous, overwhelming exercise, but should emerge as an energizing, activating, lighthearted connectedness. The bonds of gender and the bonds of sisterhood cross religious, ethnic, and cultural lines.

The positive energy of sisterhood jumps from the pages of feminist literature. A difficult challenge for me was to stop the research for this book and engage in the actual writing. As I reviewed research, each book was characterized by a delightful personal sharing by the author or authors. I, as no doubt all readers would, identified with many of the writers' observations, and reveled in the sisterhood bonds these anecdotes created. Moreover, some of the most erudite books on women's ways of knowing contained personal vignettes of gatherings in living rooms among families while the teamwork of the book evolved. The consistency of sisterhood being celebrated in each book was no accident. Each book emphasizes the immense value of networking with other women.

Women-to-Women: Change Catalysts

At the 1997 Million Women's March held in Philadelphia, one organizer commented "Now it's time that we (women) take care of ourselves." The energy that women together can project has powers of creation that knows no bounds. Connections with other women are sources of rejuvenation. You need to have sources of renewal in your life. Through connections with other women, the power of sisterhood energizes you and mobilizes you to positions of leadership.

Working women need to reach out to the resources of other women, while avoiding an anti-male perspective. Catalyzing change often requires the input of other individuals. In my own personal life, initially creating the Boston Women's Group in the mid-1970s culminated in my decision to return to doctoral studies. During my doctoral studies, networking with the nursing management staff in the Public Health Department, especially Ginger Burks, energized my dissertation efforts. At the Center of Psychological Effectiveness, the emergence of an all-women therapist team has created a supportive momentum for the changing health care market. The Women of Wisdom Power Breakfast Group, an executive women focus group, and the mentoring involvement of chief executive officer, Pat Moran for the development of this book demonstrates the empowering catalyst of women-to-women bonding and support.

Catapult yourself to an activation of your positive power by placing a priority on your sisterhood relationships. The power of sisterhood helps your transition through different and often difficult stages. In creating your own sisterhood network, you need to recognize that you are not limited to formal groups. Each of you can create a group that will meet your individual needs. Researchers of feminist professors confirmed the value of sisterhood with their article titled, "Feminism as a life raft," and a participant in the study eloquently stated, "For me, I think the answer is clear; it's other women. Other women . . . with whom I could join forces and both talk and try to change things. That makes all the difference in the world as far as I am concerned." Include sisterhood as a factor in your life. Other women can be positive power chargers in your growth and development.

The Story of Jane, Nancy and Susan

In my private practice, I remembered well the lessons of the positive catalyst of others. During one period in my practice, I was working individually with three young women. All three women were married, struggling in their careers, and filled with considerable self-doubt. Each patient had made considerable progress in resolving past issues of trauma, controlling anxieties, and gaining more effective coping strategies in her individual sessions. However, these women's statements of self-doubt were still considerable. Remembering the "catalyst of others," I created a therapy group comprised of the three women. The group was comprised of Jane, a low level manager, Susan, who had moved steadily up the corporate ladder, and Nancy, who had just emerged after motherhood with a degree and new work skills.

Jane, a striking and elegant black woman, turned heads as she walked and projected charisma. Haunted by internal self-doubt, she churned with messages of fear. The group was a catalyst for her to speak to her manager and indicate her management interests. Subsequently, Jane relocated, and was tapped for a fast track management-training program. Susan, an immigrant, was creative, intelligent, vivacious, and attractive. Often, she would retreat into her bedroom on weekends, withdrawing from the world. Susan mobilized to increase her limit-setting on the job, confront patronizing males, and speak up at executive meetings. She was promoted and became the second woman to hold an executive staff position. Nancy was an attractive, licensed professional, who was witty, thoughtful, articulate, and bright. Nancy agonized over "doing the right thing." The group experience resulted in her increasing social outreaches and risk-taking behaviors. Nancy began to take solo trips and decrease her anxiousness. Clearly, the interaction of the three women together propelled them to new level of change.

Beyond the Word

Feminism is a part of every woman's life. You are each impacted by the advocacy for equal treatment, equal opportunity, and the elimination of oppression in society. Do not allow the distortions of the media or the distortions of society to reduce your commitment to feminism. You do not have to wave a feminist banner; you do not have to behave in an adversarial manner. Feminism is constructive, proactive actions that positively impact women and men. Inequality, discrimination, and oppression have been oozing sores in the history of civilization. Each of us owes it to ourselves and to society to stop the oozing sores, heal society, and improve the quality of our lives.

You and I, in our actions, clarity of thinking, and ability to celebrate and advocate for women and their talents will always be a part of the feminist movement. Do not be persuaded from viewing yourself as a feminist because of the contamination of the word. Labels can stereotype. Understand the essence of feminism, and be a feminist in your heart. A feminist means to participate in public and private acts to increase the quality of life for women and men. You, as a liberated woman, do not fit any preconceived design. Each of us is unique, there is no one liberated woman. Psychological studies consistently report that women who hold feminist beliefs have higher self-esteem and more effective coping strategies.

You do not have to be a feminist in name—but be a feminist in thought and action. When you are a feminist in thought, you do not see any discrimination or oppression that you experience as a result of any lack of self-worth, nor do you blame yourself. Rather you recognize that it is the other person's limitations that create the behavior. You also possess a belief in your abilities and the wisdom of women, and you activate your positive power for the goals you select. You recognize that women's struggles must be seen in the context of the political and the social environment. You are not invisible any longer. You are no longer represented as a victim. You are a powerful and talented woman who shapes your personal and your professional world.

You need to consider collective, as well as personal, actions in order to have a larger impact. A critical mass of action is necessary. We possess the critical mass of numbers, now activation of positive power is needed. Women who comprise forty-six percent (46%) of the workforce, fifty-one percent (51%) of the population, and fifty-four percent (54%) of the electorate constitute less than fifteen percent (15%) of federal legislators. Clearly, Congress must change to reflect the demographics of American society. Women will limit their advancements by avoiding collective actions. If we can begin to engage in more effective actions, as in voting, women will create a momentum for major social changes. Women, with our unique wisdom, will create a more nurturing society for both women and men.

Feminism has the ability to accommodate a wide variety of voices. You need to increase your tolerance for differing opinions. By virtue of being a woman, even if political philosophies differ, you have a contribution to make. The opportunity for your voice to be heard needs to be promoted. As you mobilize to reshape society, you respect your differences, you capitalize on your similarities, and you allow the full spectrum of diversity to be heard. The principles of diversity and anti-oppression need to be etched in stone. The model for both female and male behaviors is a biopsychosocial model recognizing the new research of biology and psychological experience, and the social and political environment.

Although multiple variables—such as culture, class, age, race, and sexual orientation—impact us, your gender is central to your life. Feminist thoughts will help you mobilize your positive power, engage in appropriate initiatives to end oppression, receive equal pay and opportunity, and join in life-enhancing connections with other women and men.

Star Points

★ Feminism, as a social change agent movement, has been distorted in the media.

★ The core of feminism is unlimited options for all.

★ Divisiveness among women, both within and outside the feminist movement, is a significant power drain.

★ A variety of feminist beliefs exist on a wide spectrum.

★ Gender wars are not necessary or helpful to feminism.

★ Standards of physical attractiveness are determined by each individual.

★ Feminism does not dictate physical presentation.

★ Motherhood and feminism are compatible.

★ Working mothers enhance the emotional and financial lives of their families.

★ Psychological research reports that feminists' beliefs positively impact psychological and physical well-being.

★ Gender differences are to be respected and are best understood with a biopsychosocial model.

★ Cross-training in gender behaviors can benefit both women and men.

★ Women's studies programs make valuable contributions to both personal and societal growth.

★ Sisterhood is a powerful vehicle for maximizing your positive power.

★ Avoid aversions to the word feminism and engage in personal and collective actions for the enhancement of your own life and the world.

6

The Wisdom
of Women

"Women are the real architects of society."
—Harriet Beecher Stowe,
Author, Social Critic

Self-Acknowledgment

Women are not "one size fits all." Gender roles that place all women at one end of the spectrum opposite men are outdated. Women exist on a continuum and possess many talents and different interests. Women come in all shapes, sizes, and colors. However, women possess some unique characteristics. Women bear children, experience menopause, have more right and left brain connections, and are shaped by a combination of our biology and society. Being a woman is all that you need to be. A woman does not have to diminish her gender to exercise her positive power. In the words of choreographer Twyla Tharp, "I studied men and adapted myself to their world, I tried to emulate them. Eventually, I realized that I didn't have to 'become' a man to be powerful."

Women are beginning to celebrate themselves as women. Within United States society, a surge of the Goddess Movement is returning to celebrate women and nature. Women wisdom appreciates women's unique ways of knowing. This appreciation is not to be interpreted, however, as believing that female perceptions are better than male perceptions. Recent research has consistently demonstrated that gender differences exist between male and female perspectives. Characterizing the female way or the male way as either better or less worthy than the other gender's way is a waste of energy and time. Women and men have different perspectives that are both to be appreciated and utilized. Presently, women's unique ways of knowing have been underutilized in boardrooms, corporations, the public sector, and political leadership. The challenges of the new millennium require the utilization of the perspectives of women.

The research on the unique talents of women would fill volumes. The purpose of this chapter is not an exhaustive overview of the voluminous gender research. Rather, this chapter highlights some of the exceptional talents that you bring to both your personal and professional life. The highlighted feminine talents have been selected with the demands of the new global economy in mind. The new millennium requires both public and private organizations to stretch in new directions. Women can make significant contributions to this stretching and reengineering to prepare for the new millennium. Women's ways of knowing create exceptional savvy businesswomen who will be exceptional assets.

For too long, the male standard and the male perspective has been seen as the ideal. This androcentric viewpoint is limited. Each gender can only contribute its own perspective. Males need to develop an appreciative awareness of women's talents. Women are not to be seen as tokens or carbon copies of men that are merely packaged differently. Women are to be viewed as a separate gender bringing a unique perspective. The talents of both women and men need to be culled and combined in varying combinations to find solutions to the new challenges.

The research of Moir and Jessel discusses in detail gender differences in cognitive abilities. *Brainsex*, their provocative book stated, "Better, to welcome and exploit the complimentary differences between men and women. Women should contribute their specific female gifts rather than waste their energies in the pursuit of a sort of surrogate masculinity. A woman's greater imagination can solve intractable problems—be they professional or domestic—at one apparently intuitive stroke."

Research has consistently demonstrated that both biological and social factors contribute to gender differences. Gender differences need to be viewed as differences, not deficiencies. Situations in life vary widely. Different talents, different perceptions, and different insights are useful at different times. Situational flexibility is extremely important as the world becomes more complex and condensed both by technology and the emergence of the global economy. Organizations, utilizing the combined talents of women and men dramatically increase their range of strategies available for problem-solving. The advantage of using female and male talents has been demonstrated in the higher return to the bottom line for corporations who have eliminated the Glass Ceiling. Thus, the increasing world diversity requires increasing the diversity of approaches and the elimination of the Glass Ceiling.

Data Gatherers

Although biology is not the sole determiner of behavior, recent advances in cognitive science have increased the understanding of brain functions. Research evidence indicates that the female brain and the male brain do not work in the same manner. Studies have demonstrated that women have a larger number of connections between the right and left brain hemispheres. The right and left parts of the human brain are connected by the corpus callosum. These extra corpus callosum connections allow you to absorb more information between your brain hemispheres. There is a high probability that what is commonly known as women's intuition stems from these expanded connections between the right and left brain.

As the day-to-day knowledge gathered expands, your brain structure helps you sort the enormous masses of information in today's society. Your increased brain connections allow you to accept a wider range of sensory information. Also, your right and left brain exchanges give you an advantage in mastering foreign languages. Women's special skills for foreign languages are a major asset in this global economy.

Physiological gender differences include women having an increased number of receptive rods and cones in the retina. The increased number of rods and cones allow you to receive a wider arc of visual input. In today's technological society, visual cues are crucial. Your wider peripheral vision allows you to incorporate a larger picture. Since you can physically "see more" you collect more visual data. Your increased personal database of knowledge enhances your decision-making. Your challenge is to translate the data from your physical vision to a vision for the future.

The female socialization process assists women in being superb data gatherers. Women have been socialized not to discount emotional feelings. Thus, women are able to incorporate emotional data with factual data. Women, with their other-focused template, have antennae that gather verbal and non-verbal data. You have an enhanced ability to "read" other people and perceptively gauge multiple parameters of any situation. You key in on voice tones, facial expressions, body posture, and moods. Thus, you provide comprehensive assessments that are valuable components of effective decision-making.

Recognize how valuable your talents are. You have the ability to absorb and sort greater quantities of information, you gather more visual data, and you gather non-verbal cues and have well-honed abilities to sense emotions. Remember, comprehensive information is the key to insightful decisions. As a woman, you possess exceptional data-gathering talents.

Information Sharers

Women often create web-like structures that are useful in today's information age. Women like to be at the center and invite input from all sources. Sharing information and seeking more information from others contributes to women's abilities to communicate effectively. While a chain of command structure can still be recognized, women tend to easily bridge such structures when the need arises. Women managers are less concerned with titles and cumbersome chains of command. Women create information webs with numerous lines open to input from others. They focus on being in the middle of things and their connectedness to people facilitates their ability to amass information and sort information. Women who are in the midst of the people they manage become conduits for information, rather than information blockers. Females enjoy the spontaneous interruption that not only allows a person-to-person connection, but also creates an opportunity to gather more input.

Women have much less of a focus on the need for status that arises from following a protocol or correct channels. Once again, while women can abide lines of command, they can also easily cross over these lines to adapt to changing needs and situations. This openness to input from all sources allows more frequent brainstorming. Little fear exists that ideas will be co-opted or concerns will arise for obtaining credit for an idea— rather, the overriding need to compile effective information leads to an emphasis on communication. This information-sharing process is helpful in a rapidly changing corporate environment. The quicker an organization can incorporate information, the more responsive and effective the organization will be. The web communication structure that women prefer is an asset in today's global economy.

Flexibility

Women possess strong flexibility skills in both consideration of new ideas and adapting to different circumstances. This ability to be flexible, however, means that most women deplore stuffiness and prefer a more relaxed flexible atmosphere, and indeed thrive in it. Just as the web pattern of information-sharing allows greater information-gathering, being flexible encourages this communication. Women's societal role has trained them to be flexible—juggling multiple demands to accomplish several tasks with competing priorities. The flexibility to sense individual needs and adapt different managerial styles tailored to employee needs are managerial strengths for women. This management ability to spontaneously adapt to changing needs is an important quality for managing diverse workforces.

Women are masters of situational leadership with their well-honed human relation's skills. They adjust their style to the individuals that they supervise and the situation in which they find themselves. Women's situational flexibility is well-suited to the rapidly changing workforce.

Power Sharers

Women also are willing to share power by helping others around them. They enjoy mentoring, teaching, and are comfortable fostering employee growth. Females gain considerable pleasure in being a catalyst for the growth of others. As a result, women are interested in allowing others to succeed, and want to create an environment for their success.

Team-building and team efforts come naturally to many women. In a team situation, all members contribute value to the project, and the pride in achievement is shared among the people on the team. Women's ability to share the glory and acknowledge team involvement creates loyalty and enthusiasm in the workplace and increases employee self-esteem. Women are less concerned about who gets the credit; they are much more concerned about the goal being accomplished. Eschewing credit can be a double-edged sword, however, since women need to claim responsibility for their accomplishments in order to advance, even while their focus is more on accomplishing the goal. Women need to differentiate between sharing the achievement through recognition of the team and obtaining the necessary exposure of being the team motivator and key player in accomplishing the task.

Collaboration

Multiple researchers have found that women's preferred way of interacting is in a collaborative manner. Women readily allow themselves to appropriately seek help from others and are comfortable interacting with others. The collaborative style of women creates teamwork and consensus which is becoming the role model for managing in the new millennium.

The organizations for the future will be built on the strengths of relationships among people, rather than formal channels of authority that have guided most organizations. The management skills of collaboration that women possess will be indispensable to the growth of new millennium organizations.

Women shine in their team-building skills. They enjoy fostering cooperation, trust, and mutual respect. Women have the ability to relate to all members of the team as individuals, not just technicians. Collaboration requires that everyone be recognized and everyone be respected just by being a member of the team. The ability to share power, be flexible with impromptu brainstorming, and meld diverse information sources gives rise to a strong collaboration style. Creative and innovative work teams can be assembled and held together through strong collaborative leadership. Women's collaborative style encourages participation by all and enhances the self-worth of all members of the team. The collaborative leadership of women creates a nourishing environment for the non-hierarchical flow of information.

Women want to maintain solid relationships that will make the team work more smoothly. Women's team leadership style results in them pitching in and doing whatever it takes to move the project along, regardless of rank or hierarchy. Many times, women see their projects almost as a living child and the overall goal is the well-being of the project and their valuable employees. Women show appreciation for everyone's dedication to the project and readily recognize the importance of small, individual contributions that enable the success of the whole project. Women are comfortable with the networking tools of recognition, and often will send thank-you notes to people who helped them achieve the results.

Win-Win Negotiators

In the past, winning usually meant someone else was losing. Modern day business practices have recognized the importance of all parties in business negotiations becoming winners to some degree. This is known as the win-win situation. A negotiator can achieve these positive results by focusing on a beneficial solution, rather than gaining advantage over an opponent. Women, with their focus on connectedness and enjoyment of interpersonal interaction prefer to create an outcome of win-win. Compatible benefits are negotiated for each player. Females are much less invested in the traditional win through ensuring loss to a competitor. Victories are pursued less than accords between involved groups.

Women's openness to creativity and win-win solutions is extremely useful in our rapidly changing economy. Negotiators must bring adaptability and flexibility to the table to achieve a mutually beneficial agreement. In today's economy of merger mania, yesterday's competitor may be tomorrow's colleague. Negotiated accords can easily create bridges to partnerships.

Women enjoy utilizing their interpersonal skills to create harmonious relationships to reach an accord. Female empathy promotes seeking a positive outcome with a consideration of the interests of the other parties—negotiating benefits to all sides in a win-win process. An area where women have strength in this process is with the ability to put themselves in their competitor's shoes. Empathy for the impact of the action on others is a negotiating strength.

Women also take into consideration the human variables and diverse behaviors of the parties during negotiations. Your ability to read non-verbal cues and your astuteness in assessing human reaction is a phenomenal strength at the negotiating table. Women seek harmonious accords and are win-win negotiators.

Multitask Wizards

Women, for years, have been attending to a myriad of work activities, both in the home and at the office. Women have been juggling household tasks, demands of children, needs of spouses, business requirements, and sometimes obligations to elderly parents. For decades, women have developed well-honed experience in balancing conflicting interests, pacing themselves, and creating incredible organization systems. Women are masters at juggling diverse personalities, solving problems, and ensuring that priorities are met for a variety of needs. Women are the consummate jugglers. Anne Morrow Lindbergh said, "What a circus act we women perform every day of our lives. It puts the trapeze artist to shame."

The history of women assuming multiple roles and meeting the needs of many people with diverse personalities provided strong role models for responding flexibly to varying requests. The organizational skills and flexibility needed to cope with the demands of the new millennium are hallmarks of female behaviors. The societal demands of the new millennium require the ability to flexibly move from task to task.

Women pay attention to details and shift easily from one task to the next. Women check off items on their many lists and then create a new list. Women excel at accomplishing their projects, while ensuring nothing slips through the cracks. Women master details and savor the enjoyment of the completed task.

The mere act of handling assignments from various people in her life has conditioned women to tolerate interruptions with minimal resentment. As a woman, you have the ability to sustain an interruption and return to the task at hand. The talent of being "interruption proof" allows you a flexibility to respond to the changing demands of both your work and home environment

Managing multiple priorities is a necessary part of the business world. As the intensity of communication increases—through mail, email, telephone, fax, and personal interactions—women have to sort quickly through the burgeoning requests, all the while prioritizing and keeping the overall purpose in sight. Women's past experiences have developed these juggling and filtering strengths, and you bring these developed strengths to the business world. Women are multitask wizards of balancing and satisfying multiple priorities—key skills for the new millennium.

Change Tolerant

Women have always needed to quickly change focus to respond to demands from different sources. The ability to balance the priorities requires women to be sufficiently flexible to move quickly between different tasks. Add to this the ability of women to be able to tolerate ambiguity. Clear direction isn't always available, and women have rarely had the time or luxury to completely and unambiguously understand all assignments thrust on them. You gather sufficient information to start, and fill in the gaps as you go. Your increased flexibility and ability to sort large amounts of data quickly fosters an increased comfort with change.

Technology is causing change to occur faster and faster as you enter the new millennium, and women's responsiveness to change is a key skill. Whether it is the ability to adapt to the new technology or the interruptions that technology brings, women's tolerance of change is an important trait.

While women are change tolerant, you may also be intolerant of inflexibility. Many times corporations may lose the talent of women due to the organization's inability to change. A recent article in the *American Psychological Monitor* stated, "Many companies lose effective women leaders because they refuse to make changes that women want to make." Women not only are change tolerant, you are also innovators who want to create change in your companies. If the corporation is unresponsive, you may relocate to a more progressive company. This can be extremely costly for corporations. The cost of replacing a seasoned manager or professional averages one hundred fifty to one hundred ninety-three percent (150-193%) of their annual salary. The inability of corporations to respond to the innovative changes recommended by women may be a significant factor in the phenomenal increase in women entrepreneurs.

Team Leadership

Women's team management style, openness to questioning, and open-ended thinking creates an environment that allows more innovation and creativity. The concept that there are no wrong answers promotes a brainstorming process to reach the desired goal. Brainstorming encourages your creativity and generates positive energy, which is much needed in today's global economy. Women, as team managers, inspire employees to creative heights. The team management style of women creates opportunity for employees, rather than imposing control on workers. The team leadership role of women is as involved leaders, participating as a productive part of the work-team, rather than acting as a distant supervising entity.

Women team leaders are part of the daily flow, and energize their team. Women enjoy being teachers and empowering their employees to problem-solve independently.

Team leadership is consistent with the power-with style. Organizational research studies have shown that women rank higher in their ability to get the best from their employees and to create atmospheres of company integrity and enthusiasm. The collaborative information-gathering, flexibility, and open style of women has often been described as being a transformational leader. Transformational leadership and interactive leadership both are terms that have been used to describe women's management skills. Women recognize employee needs, tap their potential, and foster a continual development of employee skills. Women managers develop the talents of the employees and maximize their productivity.

Innovators

For all of the reasons previously discussed—information-sharing, flexibility, collaboration, tolerance to change—women have tended to become innovators. Women tend to rank higher in being able to intellectually stimulate their employees and encourage "out-of-the-box" thinking. Their openness to all input allows leaps in thinking. You challenge your employees to look at problems from new and unique perspectives.

Women often consider several solutions for achieving a goal. Societal experiences have allowed women to develop the flexibility to accept innovative ways of getting the job done. Boundaries and limits are set, but all possibilities within the boundaries can be considered. These traits allow you to frequently dismiss the notion of one correct answer, and challenge your employees to develop new answers.

You are also an innovator and visionary because you foster an increased responsibility to the world at large. Your concern for others—now called by marketers "Female Think", helps companies develop corporate visions to direct a portion of profits to improve society. The concept of Female Think means women look for the ongoing connection in any deal—the future relationships formed by any negotiation or solution. In the large picture, you want to make the world a better place for those that follow and your children. Your concern with world welfare causes you to have a global focus, which is well-suited to today's economy. Women become visionary leaders, as they want to make a difference, not only for their organization, but also for the world at large.

Integrators

Women, with their antenna reaching in many directions to gather data, develop a momentum to create consensus. Women's behavioral momentum to reach a consensus fosters integration. Women assess multiple variables and fit the variables together, similar to pieces of a puzzle, developing an integrated whole. Women have a minimal tolerance for fragmentation and consistently coach their employees to develop an integrated perspective.

Women possess a psychological perspective to create webs of inclusion. You enjoy the mutuality of relationships. As a result, you integrate multiple resources to achieve your project's objectives. You maintain an openness to integrate new people, new ideas, and new approaches.

Not only do you integrate on the macro level, you integrate on the micro level. Your management style is to consider both personal and business variables in utilizing the talents of your work team. The consideration you demonstrate to your employees in understanding them as individuals builds strong loyalty. Your respect for their contributions and your integration of their ideas into projects energizes your work team. Loyalty and productive energy are valuable assets for all work environments.

Tap Your Talents

Your talents are numerous. This chapter has featured and highlighted just a few of the ways that you contribute to the workplace. You want to bring your unique talents to the table with a sense of assurance, utilizing your positive power. The research is clear that your collaborative ways and team leadership have already begun to transform the workplace. As you enter your next negotiation for a raise, as you develop your strategic career plan, as you establish your goals, do not doubt for a minute the talent that you bring to your company. For too long, women have allowed themselves to be held back by self-doubt, self-questioning, and by feelings of powerlessness. The data is clear—women's unique wisdom can only catapult you to unlimited success.

Star Points

★ Women and men contribute different talents.

★ Women's wisdom is to be celebrated.

★ The brain structure of women allows them to be superb gatherers of data.

★ Women with their enhanced communication skills facilitate information-sharing.

★ Women thrive on the ability to be flexible.

★ Women with their focus on connections with others willingly share power and credit.

★ Women's preferred way of interacting is a collaborative style.

★ Women's collaborative style of interaction and empathy allows them to shine in win-win negotiating.

★ Socialization practices have developed in women the ability to be multitask wizards.

★ Women can be powerful change agents.

★ Women's enjoyment of teaching and mentoring employees creates a transformational style of leadership also called team leadership.

★ Women's global perspective of change stimulates them to be innovative visionaries.

★ Women prefer consensus-building and integrate information, talent and abilities into powerful teams.

★ Women possess unique talents that will continue to shine in the new millennium.

7

Star
Power

"If (women) understood and exercised their
power they could remake the world."
—*Emily Taft-Douglas, Congresswoman*

Creating Versus Waiting

Women, both personally and developmentally, are past the stage where they need to wait for permission. On International Woman's Day, March 8, 1998, a symposium was held titled "Women of the World of Enterprise: Possibilities and Challenges." During the symposium, Italian Chamber of Commerce spokesperson Belisario Capocci stated, "The twenty-first century will be the Century of the Woman."

Women possess the power of numbers and the power of economics. Women are mobilizing to create an agenda of utilizing all of the talents of both women and men to enhance competitiveness in the new global economy. A key element will be to elect more females to political positions, allowing society to benefit from both female and male input. The perspective of creating opportunities, rather than waiting to be called or waiting to be asked, is an important mental shift.

How can you create? How can you take the initiative? Do you hold onto the myth that women are fearful, and that women have difficulty coping with success? If you hold a belief that initiative is difficult, you need to challenge your thinking with the hard data of research.

A research study by Dr. Paludi reported that the female fear of success taps a cultural stereotype rather than a female intrapsychic motivational problem. A study by Pfost and Fury discussed that women's intrapsychic desires for success and achievement were negatively impacted by women fearing social isolation. The business environment today removes these isolation fears. Women are now forty-six percent (46%) of the workforce and rapidly becoming the majority. Women are no longer alone. Recognize that now, and in the future, you gain multiple networking opportunities with other women and increased social contact as you strive for success and achievement.

The only limit to your ability is your own lack of initiatives. In the words of Madeline Kunin, former governor of Vermont, "Women need to see themselves as individuals creating change. That is what political and economic power is all about: having a voice, being able to shape the future. Women's absence from decision-making positions has deprived the country of a necessary perspective."

Partnership Versus Adversaries

Moir and Jessel in *Brainsex* made an astute observation, "It would be a sad reflection on the intelligence of the world of work if, having understood the separate strengths and strategies that men and women bring to bear, it ignored the prudence of combining them." Years of research substantiate that women and men bring complimentary skills to the table. The effective merger of female and male skills will yield the best results.

An encouraging gender relation's project, begun in 1993, is underway at the Wellesley Center for Women, Stone Research Center. The project included a comprehensive canvassing of over twenty thousand individuals from all walks of life. Results noted a strong movement for both women and men to create "growth fostering relationships," which will create effective partnerships. The goal is to create equitable partnerships between women and men. These partnerships will be built on an appreciation of differences and tap into the considerable talents of both parties.

The new millennium does not need a patriarchy or a matriarchy—
it needs a partnership of women and men. Superiority theories
throughout history have destroyed civilizations. Women and men need
to learn and understand each other's styles with mutual respect. The
best strategy is to take into account the differences between women and
men, adjust appropriately, and learn. Women and men need to link together in a spirit of collaboration. Neither female nor male gives up their
individual uniqueness. Rather, women and men will collaborate together
as individuals bringing similar and different talents to bear. The collaborative partnership between women and men is in the process of evolving.
The demands of the global economy and the expanding roles of women
will hasten the arrival of this collaborative partnership.

Support Versus Divisiveness

Women attacking women, quibbling among themselves, back-stab-
bing each other—this behavior drains energy from themselves and
others. Women need to be united in sisterhood to offer each other mutual support in order to move beyond the Glass Ceiling. Women need to
support women. You need to mentor each other. For years, present leaders form strong mentoring relationships with protegées who "pick their
brains" and receive a legacy of life information.

A fascinating example of women supporting and mentoring women
occurred in Australia. The Business Matrix was established by the Victo-
rian Woman's Trust and Woman's Enterprise Connection and received
public funding. Business Matrix is a set of office suites where the tenants
were provided with more than just office space. The tenants of the Business Matrix were provided management assistance, marketing assistance,
financial and legal advice, networks, and informal mentoring links. The
concept of the Business Matrix is a fascinating business idea. The tenants of the Business Matrix were chosen to create cross-referrals and
establish a support network for business opportunities. Although businesswomen received preference in the access to the business suites,
men were not excluded. This new collaborative enterprise is a strong
statement that supportiveness is also good business.

Supportiveness also has the dimensions of creating role models. Oprah Winfrey is making major contributions to creating new opportunities for women and changing the culture. The honesty and dignity with which she has disclosed some of her life issues has been encouraging to millions of women. In my practice, I have seen hundreds of women discuss her shows in detail and be motivated to maintain personal gratitude journals. The incredible impact of Oprah is reflected in the new term "The Oprah Effect," which means professionals who are media friendly. More professionals need to have a media profile to communicate research results and dispel gender myths.

Women, and especially feminist scholars, need to consider their position on media friendliness. The media can wield tremendous power. For too long women's strengths, abilities, power, and utilization of power have been misunderstood and distorted. You can contribute to accurate information about women. The importance of the media in shaping culture will increase in the new millennium. Women's Media Watch Project of Standards and Accuracy in Reporting is working diligently to monitor media representations of women. In the political arena, The Women's Research and Education Institute (WREI) provides information, research, and policy analysis to the members of Congress to support the equity movement for women. Over the years, WREI has been a source of reliable information. WREI helps promote legislative decision-making based on quality information. Moreover, the organization scrutinizes public policies and encourages the development of policies that recognize the circumstances of women and their families. These and other organizations are trying to set the record straight. Women in the real world, not the myths, need to be presented. You need to be media friendly and serve as a role model.

Supportiveness also encompasses supporting candidates for office. Over the years, from my League of Women Voter days in the 1970s, through anchoring the *Sunday League Radio Program* in the Boston, Massachusetts area, through hundreds of hours in therapy with female and male patients, and through the research for this book—all has compelled me to strongly advocate for the support of women candidates. Yes, I believe that you should support a woman just because she is a woman. Even if a woman's political agenda is different than your own agenda, women need to be represented in more equal numbers in political positions. Politics is the one area where a screaming disparity exists between the proportions of women in the population and the proportion of women in political leadership positions. As discussed earlier, women are fifty-one percent (51%) of the population but represent less than fifteen percent (15%) of the members of Congress. Until elected women in Congress reflect the demographic profile of the country, the United States does not have a representative democracy.

Women's voices need to be added to the political leadership of this country and of the world. Especially with our growing knowledge about the difference between women and men, the complimentary talents of both need to be activated. In the book *Women In Power*, California Congresswoman Nancy Pelosi stated, "Power is not anything that anybody has given away in the history of the world. I tell women all the time that if you want it, you have to go for it and you have to be very serious about getting it and holding it. It's not anything anti-woman or anything else. It's just that men don't want to give up their power to another man or to a woman." Political positions of leadership are essential to ensure appropriate legal rights and to help sculpt the future of society. Women's unique talents are desperately needed in the political arena.

The fascinating book by Linda Witt, *Running As A Woman: Gender and Power in American Politics*, recounts the history of women in the political arena. The story behind the 1994 election cycle demonstrated that the road has been paved for women to finance campaigns and run for political office. Once again in 1998, the number of women in the House of Representatives increased, but not enough. Women have an excellent track record of winning open seat elections. However, more women candidates are needed. Hillary Clinton encourages the activation of women power with her statement, "Empowerment of women is as critical for a vibrant democracy as are issues like trade, diplomacy, and national security." Whether you exercise your right to vote, financially support a female candidate, volunteer time for a political candidate, write letters to editors on political issues, lobby for a delegate seat within your political party, or run for office yourself, political involvement is a key ingredient to moving beyond the Glass Ceiling and reshaping society.

The supportiveness of women will take on multiple dimensions. Support each other as mentors, business colleagues, role models, and as politicians. Women connecting to women will create a web of inclusion encompassing the diversity that exists among womankind. Women of Wisdom celebrate other women. Women will move beyond the Glass Ceiling—together—in a swelling momentum of initiatives, energies, and positive powers.

A Victory Parade

The accomplishments of women are numerous. Even though much work remains to move beyond the Glass Ceiling, there needs to be a positive focus on women's achievements. It is not too early for women to hold a "victory parade."

The changes in opportunities for women have been phenomenal, yet in life there is always more room for improvement. As a clinical psychologist, part of my professional responsibility is to assess the appropriate time for a patient's clinical discharge. At the time of clinical discharge, patients have not reached one hundred percent (100%) of their therapy goals. The timing of clinical discharge is when the patient has resolved seventy percent (70%) to eighty percent (80%) of their treatment goals. Just so, women also need to control their perfectionist tendencies, and begin to acknowledge their substantial gains. Too frequently, my female patients minimize their significant gains and focus on what still needs to be accomplished. Women need training to acknowledge their gains and also to learn how to "toot their own horn." The following statistics support the premise that *now* is the time for women to conduct a "victory parade."

First, women hold many different positions in United States society and represent a powerful force. Research conducted by Catalyst found that " . . . women have attained a critical mass in middle management, especially in the service industries." Additional Catalyst statistics found that while in 1982 there were 0.62 white female professionals for every white male, a decade later there were 0.94 white female professionals for every white male. Between 1982 and 1992, black women were found to be the fastest growing group of managers, with one hundred and twenty-five percent (125%) increase in management positions. Statistics are numerous on the critical mass of women today. Women are fifty-six percent (56%) of students in higher education, eighty-six percent (86%) of women age 15–64 are employed, forty-six percent (46%) of the entire United States' workforce are women, and women are fifty-one percent (51%) of the American population. Women now constitute a critical mass that can ignite exciting social changes. In the new millennium, the critical mass of women will increase, women are projected by the U.S. Department of Labor to represent forty-eight percent (48%) of the labor force in 2005. The following figure projects the age distribution of female labor in the new millennium.

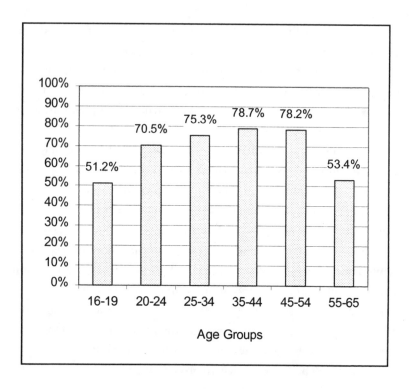

Figure I

U.S. Department of Labor Force
Participant Rates for Women by Age Group

Projected 2000

Women are "having it all" with careers, children, and marriage. A recent poll reported eighty-two percent (82%) of women and eighty-three percent (83%) of men were enjoying their lives. The myth needs to be dispelled that women activate their careers and put their personal lives at peril. At the same time that women are increasing their involvement in the work force, divorces are decreasing, and fathers are increasing their role in sharing parental responsibilities and joys. Working women keep families together—not pull them apart. The working woman in 1994, contributed fifty-six percent (56%) of family income among black couples, and contributed forty-seven percent (47%) of income among white couples. Women are welcome and necessary participants in the economic flow of the family. Not only are women necessary and welcome participants in their own economic welfare and the welfare of their families, the majority of women of all ages work. Women, especially mothers, need to let go of "mother guilt" and recognize that in today's society working is the norm. Accept your working role with enthusiasm and take pride in your contributions to the family. Acceptance is crucial to decreasing psychological turmoil and allowing inner peace.

Not only are women economic assets, women are beginning to shape policy and provide valuable leadership. Women need support and coaching, which men have always received, to assume positions of power with comfort and clarity. The statistics highlighted graphically in this section demonstrate the repositioning of women as business leaders. As women expand their utilization of power, this trend will continue to increase. Women are accumulating the work experience and are completing professional education programs. The acquisition of positive power lessons will propel managerial advancement even faster.

The Women's Research and Education Institute (WREI), documented the phenomenal impact of women acquiring education, noting that in the 1990s women constitute the majority of full-time and part-time students in institutes of higher learning. A signature moment came in June of 1995 when, for the first time in the one hundred and ninety-three-year history of West Point, the valedictorian of the graduating class was a woman! Women are a valuable talent pool. Women not only are appearing in our educational institutions as students, but women presidencies of U.S. colleges and universities have more than tripled in the last twenty years. Women's climb up the professional ladder has been fueled by increased attendance and graduation from universities and colleges, including degree programs as shown in Figure II.

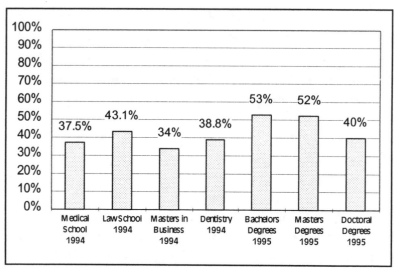

Figure II

Female Percentage of Total Degree Graduates

1994-1995

Entrepreneurs are on the same upward trend. In 1987, women owned fewer than five percent (5%) of United States businesses. However, by the mid-1990s, more than thirty-eight percent (38%) of entrepreneurs were women, and the figure is growing. Women are projected to be fifty percent (50%) of entrepreneurs by the new millennium. Women are opening businesses at *twice* the rate of men. In 1996, women owned 7.7 million companies in the United States, an increase from 4.5 million companies in 1987. The National Foundation for Women Business Owners reported that women-owned businesses employ one in five company workers in the United States and generate nearly $2.3 trillion in revenues. Women-owned businesses employ more people than all the Fortune 500 companies combined!

The U.S. Small Business Administration (SBA), continues the exciting news of women's accomplishments. The SBA touts women achievements noting, for women-owned companies with one hundred plus workers, employment increased by one hundred fifty-eight percent

(158%)—more than double the rate of all U.S. firms of similar size. Employment growth in women-owned businesses exceeds the national average in nearly every region of the country, and in nearly every major industry. In 1998, the SBA licensed the first two women-owned venture capital companies. Both companies will focus lending efforts toward women-owned firms. The two companies are Capital Across America of Nashville, Tennessee and Women's Growth Capital Fund of Washington, D.C. Clearly, women are displaying exciting initiative in creating new companies and shaping their own destiny. The following figure demonstrates the economic power of women-owned businesses.

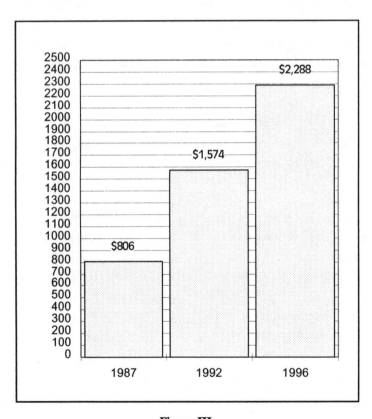

Figure III

Sales in Billion $ by Women-Owned Firms

Economic changes are also reflected in a comparison of salary differentials. Although the average working woman still only earns seventy-two percent (72%) of every dollar that the average working man earns, this discrepancy changes when you review compensation for similar work. In comparing similar jobs, we find that the average 1995 salary gap for women had narrowed from seventy-five percent (75%) of what men earned decades earlier to eighty-five percent (85%) to ninety-five percent (95%) of men's salaries. The sixty-seven percent (67%) of United States women now in administrative and managerial positions places the United States in the top ten percent (10%) of countries worldwide for women in upper level positions. In 1997, eighty-four percent (84%) of all Fortune 500 companies had at least one woman director. These statistics strongly reflect the gains that women have made economically, educationally, and in leadership. Sakiko Fukuda-Parr, keynote speaker at the fifth Global Summit of Women stated, "The growing economic power and influence of women-owned businesses are changing the shape of the global economy."

Statistics can help paint the picture, however, statistics cannot reflect the richness of human experience. Striking examples of the distance society has traveled in recognizing the contributions of women can be found by listening to any news program. If one compares the news commentary from the 1940s or 1950s to the current commentary of the late 1990s, one cannot help but see the emergence of strong female leaders in many news stories. Two women are now on the Supreme Court: Sandra Day O'Connor and Ruth Bader-Ginsburg. In 1981, Jean Kirkpatrick became the first Ambassador to the United Nations. Two years later, Sally Ride was the first American woman astronaut, and dozens have followed. The following year, Geraldine Ferraro was the first female vice-president candidate. In 1990, Antonia Novello was the first woman surgeon general. Janet Reno, in 1993, was the first woman attorney general, and, in 1997, Madeline Albright was the first woman secretary of state.

The political arena is one area where women need to increase their participation as elected leaders in the new millennium. Once women run for office, they have a strong success rate. Over half the females who ran for statewide office in 1990 won. Despite women now being fifty-one percent (51%) of the population, the number of female State Legislators in 1997 was only twenty-two percent (22%), Federal Legislators was only eleven percent (11%). Although this is certainly an increase from the eight percent (8%) present in the 1975 Congress, the growing number still does not reflect the population distribution. The bell-weather election of women was the 1994 national United States election, which increased female political representation significantly. In that year, the House saw forty-eight women being elected, including thirteen women of color. Two years later the trend was continuing, and in 1996, fifty-one women were elected, thirty-five Democrats and sixteen Republicans. In 1998, the political gains are not keeping pace with educational statistics and the statistics of women-owned businesses. The 1998 national election returns maintained nine women in the Senate and increased women power in the House to fifty-six votes. The proportion of elected women needs to increase dramatically to reflect population demographics. Clearly, mobilizing to elect women to Congress is a top priority.

Women need to assume their power, and recognize that they are the majority. The opportunities for women are viewed as greater now than they have ever been. As the majority, women have tremendous potential for changing social policy, economic trends, and the quality of life of society. Women have unique qualities that can create a world order surpassing the current world order. As you approach the new millennium, you need to take time to reflect on past accomplishments carefully and strategically decide your path for the future.

Moving Beyond

The synergy of women growing, stretching and creating new frontiers is exciting. Finish this book with your new action plan ready to be activated. Women, although not fully liberated, are transforming the world. A critical mass of women and like-minded men now exist who recognize the value of collaboration among women and men. As you move forward to beyond the Glass Ceiling, take your new positive power skills and wisdom, and relish the company of other women who are headed in the same direction. Know that you are not alone—others tread the same path and more will follow. *Shine brightly and affirm yourself daily.*

- ◁ I use my positive power for life enhancement.
- ◁ I support and celebrate the talents of other women.
- ◁ I reject limiting labels.
- ◁ I collaborate with men with mutual respect.
- ◁ I celebrate my uniqueness as a woman and define for myself how I "star" in my life.

Star Points

★ Women possess the power of numbers and the power of economics to generate significant societal change.

★ Women and men need to work together to establish productive, collaborative relationships.

★ Woman-to-woman networking and mentoring are crucial ingredients to success.

★ Women need to hold a "victory parade" for their significant achievements and contributions to both their families and to society.

★ Women entrepreneurs are experiencing significant successes.

★ Women-owned businesses employ one out of every five workers.

★ An important focus for the new millennium is to increase female representation in political office.

★ Women need to acknowledge their significant accomplishments and become "stars".

★ Women "stars" will move beyond the Glass Ceiling and the Glass Ceiling will become a historical artifact.

★ Developing your "star plan" is the next step on your life journey.

AFTERWORD

Feminism. The Feminist Movement. The First Wave. The Second Wave. The Third Wave. Power. Wisdom. The Glass Ceiling. What is this all about? I'm completely amazed how women have had to create terms for the REALITY in which they have lived. When I first read this book, I found myself reflecting back on my younger years when I was the East Coast Surfing Champion for Women, where courage, risk-taking, positioning and flexibility became the foundation from which I would build future success. The further I read, the more I realized that both the Feminist Movement and surfing had something in common; they both have three waves. In surfing, waves only develop in sets of three and you start out by learning how to "position yourself" on the First Wave, just as you would early on in a new career. As you develop your skills and abilities, you move on to riding the Second Wave which presents greater challenges, and finally, you choose to master the toughest wave of all...the third and final Wave. The Third Wave is the biggest, the longest and most difficult to master. But like many choices we make in life, there is a risk factor to consider. Whether you make a decision to ride the *right* wave or make the *right* career move, planning your strategy every step of the way is critical. I've been riding the waves of life for over forty years now, and through focused dedication, planning, and continuous growth, I have pioneered my own path that connects to a *powerful purpose.* One thing I do know is that connecting to a *powerful purpose* is important for all of us. "Power & Wisdom, The New Path for Women" identifies a basic premise for all stages of professional and personal growth that women experience. And now for the first time, that basic premise is outlined for you through a set of **Power Lessons** to help you master those skills, abilities and behaviors needed to move *beyond the Glass Ceiling.*

Like many of you, I have not followed the history of the Feminist Movement. Quite frankly, after reading this book, I now see that I was living it every step of the way. I grew up wanting to be different; to be better. This desire turned into initiative that would play a strong role in my overall formula for success. At the age of sixteen, I left home and became completely independent. It wasn't until my career began to blossom that I began to experience for myself the many challenges successful working women face.

As a successful business woman today, I can tell you that *Power and Wisdom, The New Path for Women* is not just about women, it's about YOU. You have no limitations, unless you make them. In our business and personal lives, we will always have chaos. But, you can reshape or change anything you want. You can transform your life through your own personal strength and confidence. You are in control of your own destiny. *This is not always easy.* Taking ownership of the choices you make in life is the first step in changing the direction of your future. So why not pioneer your own effort? Pioneering is risky, but don't forget the old saying (which I have found to be very true), "Successful people take risks." In order to grow effectively and implement positive change, you must first remove all the barriers that impact your talents. You must consider every day as a new experience, be flexible enough to change, and strong enough to make decisions that will help you shape your environment, regardless of the roadblocks you may encounter.

Let's face it, women are multi-talented individuals, and women and men living and working together have complimentary qualities. If known and understood, these qualities can be used to achieve greater success. *Power and Wisdom, The New Path for Women* is about reality and equal opportunities for both women and men. It's about growth, achievement, self-awareness and self-development. It's about the future. Developing, growing and mastering power and wisdom is a process that unfolds over time through ownership of self-development and capitalizing on life experiences. Dr. Marotta's book will guide you in those areas you choose to master for the long run. Remember, mastery provides you with the opportunity to give back to others through mentoring or coaching, and as we know, wisdom gained and shared can be a valuable lesson for us all.

On a business front, we must continue to evaluate where we are and where we are going, as we are constantly faced with a fast-paced, global economy in an ever-changing era. Smart corporations around the country will realize over time that preventing women from "Moving Beyond the Glass Ceiling" could inhibit their overall performance and jeopardize a clearer, more balanced vision for the future. This realization has already begun by several forward-thinking organizations across the U.S. and will ultimately result in a win-win for women, men and shareholders.

And on a more personal and passionate note, I encourage you to continue to set goals beyond your dreams. Seek out new opportunities to lead the future, to pave the way to success for both women and men. Have no trepidation. As you develop a clearer vision and new mindset, you will recognize that the rules aren't any different now than in the past. We make the rules. We have choices. We are in control of our own behaviors, actions and decisions.

Finally, let me leave you with these thoughts...

Consider yourself a Master Artist with a blank canvas in front of you. This canvas represents your future. You have a set of brushes and paints and with every stroke you take you begin to turn your vision into reality. The background you have just painted begins to shape your vision of success, of hope, of promise, for your future. Some people use black and white paints, some use color. Some use oils, some use water paints that wash away. What will you choose? Developing your own internal center and building upon those areas in your life that have prevented you from **moving beyond your *own* Glass Ceiling** will help you build the power and wisdom you need for future growth and success in your career and your personal life. Finding that successful balance is key.

Remember, you are the scorekeeper. Have no lingering doubts about the direction you choose and be confident with your decisions. You too can ride the waves of change, and experience and share with others the power and wisdom you have gained through your own life experiences.

Afterword

I challenge you to utilize the Power Lessons in this book to master the skills you need. Go ahead, take a good look inside yourself, reflect on the past and take ownership to shape your future—*beyond the Glass Ceiling.*

Good luck and special thanks and appreciation to Dr. Priscilla Marotta for spending countless hours building this valuable document for all to read. No doubt, the time is now, and the reality is here for all of us to embrace the future and lead the way for others to follow . . . women and men alike.

Holly C. Giertz
Vice President
JM&A Group, a JM Family Enterprises, Inc. Company

Executive Profile, Holly C. Giertz

Holly C. Giertz is Vice President for JM&A Group, a JM Family Enterprises, Inc. Company. As one of JM Family's core businesses, JM&A Group provides finance and insurance products and services to automobile dealerships throughout the country. Ranked by *Forbes* magazine as the twenty-second largest privately held corporation in the United States, JM Family Enterprises, Inc. is a diversified automotive corporation whose principal businesses focus on vehicle distribution and processing, financial and warranty services, and insurance activities.

In 1996, Holly began working with JM&A Group as Manager for Market Planning & Development; six months into her career she was promoted to Director of Marketing, and now as Vice President is responsible for Marketing, Sales Support & Customer Service, which focuses on supporting JM&A's clients and potential customers nationally. She also has responsibility for Corporate Development and Human Resources, which includes organizational development initiatives that are crucial to the company's continued short and long-term growth.

Prior to joining JM&A, Holly worked for Citicorp in their Mortgage and Consumer Banking Divisions from 1981 to 1993, where she earned eight promotions during her twelve-year tenure, including Vice President for Citibank of Florida, responsible for nineteen banks and one hundred and twenty employees. From 1993 to 1996, Holly was Regional Director for Olsten Corporation (the largest temporary staffing company in North America) responsible for Sales, Marketing and Strategic Business Initiatives for Florida.

Holly attended the University of Virginia where she earned a Graduate Degree in Retail Bank Management sponsored by the Consumer Bankers Association, holds an active Real Estate Brokers license, Mortgage Brokers license, 218 Life Insurance license, is a member of the Consumer Bankers Association, Florida Association of Realtors, National Association of Mortgage Brokers and National Association of Female Executives. She is a member of the Women of Wisdom Power Breakfast Group and was recently selected as an honored member of International Who's Who of Professionals for the year 1998.

She and her husband, Dave, live in Fort Lauderdale and have one son.

Appendix

Suggested Readings & Resources

Bingham, Mindy and Sandy Stryker. (1995). *Things Will be Different for My Daughter.* New York, NY: Penguin Books.

Cantor, Dorothy W., & Bernay, Toni. (1992). *Women in Power: The Secrets of Leadership.* New York, NY: Houghton Mifflin Company.

Clegg, Eileen M., & Swartz, Susan. (1997). *Goodbye Good Girl.* Oakland, CA: New Harbinger Publications, Inc.

Crosby, Faye J. (1991). *Juggling.* New York, NY: The Free Press.

Friedan, Betty. (1997). *Beyond Gender.* Baltimore, MD: The John Hopkins University Press.

Girls Incorporated. Materials and Programs. 212-509-2000. www.girlsinc.org

Godfrey, Joline. (1995). *No More Frogs to Kiss: 99 Ways to Give Economic Power to Girls.* New York, NY.Harper Collins.

Helgesen, Sally. (1990). *The Female Advantage.* New York, NY: Doubleday.

Horner, Althea J. (1989). *The Wish for Power and the Fear of Having It.* New York, NY: Jason Aaronson.

Lehrman, Karen. (1997). *The Lipstick Proviso: Women, Sex & Power in the Real World.* New York, NY: Doubleday.

Lerner-Robbins, Helene. (1996). *Our Power As Women: The Wisdom and Strategies of Highly Successful Women.* Berkeley, CA: Conari Press.

Miller, Jean Baker. (1986). *toward a new psychology of woman.* Boston, MA: Beacon Press.

Mindell, Phyllis. (1995). *A Woman's Guide to the Language of Success: Communicating with Confidence and Power.* Paramus, NJ: Prentice Hall.

Moir, Anne & Jessel, David. (1989). *Brain Sex: The Real Differences Between Men and Women.* New York, NY: Dell Publishing.

Reid-Merritt, Patricia. (1996). *Sister Power: How Phenomenal Black Women are Rising to the Top.* New York, NY: John Wiley & Sons, Inc.

Resource for Girls and Young Women Catalog. 800-360-1761. www.pennypaine.com

Rosener, Judy B. (1995). *America's Competitive Secret: Women Managers.* New York, NY: Oxford University Press.

Tannen, Deborah. (1994). *Talking from 9 to 5 : Women and Men in the Workplace: Language, Sex and Power.* New York, NY: Avon Books.

The Glass Paines Project. Art Exhibit. Trish Baines. 415-541-5660.

Webster, E. Carol. (1993). *Success Management.* Pompano Beach, FL: Printing Corporation of the Americas, Inc.

Walker, Rebecca (ed.). (1995). *to be real.* New York, NY: Doubleday.

Wolf, Naomi. (1993). *Fire with Fire: The New Female Power and How To Use It.* New York, NY: Random House, Inc.

1. **About Women, Inc.,** 33 Broad Street, Boston, MA 02109, (617) 723-4337 Fax (617) 723-7107 - About Women is a publishing organization dedicated to providing companies with demographic information about women. *About Women & Marketing* is their monthly newsletter.

2. **Altrusa International, Inc.,** 332 South Michigan Avenue, Chicago, IL 60604, (312) 427-4410, Fax (312) 427-8521 - An international organization dedicated to the service of others. Members come together to provide expertise to improve their communities. *The Altrusa Accent* is the organization's quarterly publication.

3. **American Association of Family and Consumer Sciences,** 1555 King Street, Alexandria, VA 22314, (703) 706-4600, Fax (703) 706-4663 - AAFCS's mission is to improve the well-being of families and individuals. The AAFCS publishes the *Journal of Family and Consumer Sciences* and *Family and Consumer Sciences Research Journal.* Additionally, AAFCS publishes a newsletter entitled, *AAFCS Action.*

4. **American Association of University Women,** 1111 16th Street, NW, Washington, D.C. 20036, (202) 785-7700, Fax (202) 872-1425, **http://www.aauw.org** - AAUW is the nation's leading advocate for education and equity for women and girls. *AAUW Outlook* is a quarterly membership magazine. *Action Alert* is the monthly public policy newsletter.

5. **American Association of Women Podiatrists,** 5900 Princess Garden Parkway, Suite 400, Lanham, MD 20706, (301) 577-4464 Fax (614) 891-4141 - AAWP provides members with networking and growth potential to enhance their careers and personal lives. They publish a quarterly newsletter.

6. **American Business Women's Association,** 9100 Ward Parkway, Kansas City, MO 64114-0728, (816) 361-6621, Fax (816) 361-4991, **http://www.abwahq.org** - ABWA brings together business women of diverse occupations. ABWA publishes a bi-monthly newsletter nationally and state chapter newsletters.

7. **American Business Women International,** P.O. Box 1137, Palm Desert, CA 92260, (760) 324-1372, **http://www.abwiworld.com/** - ABWI is a non-profit organization created to encourage and support business women involved or interested in international trade opportunities.

8. **American Medical Women's Association,** 801 North Fairfax Street, Suite 400, Alexandria, VA 22314, (703) 838-0500, Fax (703) 549-3864 - AMWA is a national organization dedicated to promoting women's health care and to improving the professional development of its members. AMWA publishes a medical education newsletter.

9. **American News Women's Club,** 1607 22nd Street, NW, Washington, DC 20008, (202) 332-6770 Fax (202) 265-6477 - ANWC reflects the rapidly changing news industry and wider range of employment opportunities for today's women, and provides assistance and encouragement in their professional development and community endeavors. Publishes a monthly newsletter.

10. **American Nurses Association**, 600 Maryland Avenue, NW, Suite 100 West, Washington, DC 20024-2571, (202) 651-7000, Fax (202) 651-7001 - ANA is dedicated to bringing together nursing and health assistance professionals. The ANA is also involved with new legislative and congressional developments. The ANA produces several publications including *Capital Update, The American Nurse, CHN Communique, CNR, Cultural Connections,* and others.

11. **American Society of Women Accountants**, 60 Revere Drive,Suite 500, Northbrook, IL 60062, (800) 326-2163, Fax (847) 480-9282, **http://www.aswa.org** - ASWA promotes women in the field of accounting. ASWA publishes *The Edge,* a national newsletter for all members. A newsletter for chapter officers is also published.

12. **American Women in Radio and Television,** 1650 Tysons Boulevard, Suite 200, McLean, VA 22102, (703) 506-3290, Fax (703) 506-3266 - AWRT is a non-profit organization advancing women in the electronic media. AWRT publishes a bi-monthly national newsletter *News and Views.*

13. **American Women's Economic Development Corporation**, 71 Vanderbilt Ave., Suite 320, New York, NY 10169, (212) 692-9100, Fax (212) 692-9296 - Trains and counsels women to be successful entrepreneurs.

14. **Association for Women in Communications,** Seven Commerce Center, 1244 Ritchie Highway, Suite 6, Arnold, MD 21012, (410) 544-7442, Fax (410) 544-4640, **http://www.WOMCOM.org** - AWP has members in the fields of print and broadcast journalism, public relations, marketing, business and association communications, advertising, magazine and book publishing, technical writing, communications education and law, photojournalism, film and design. The organization publishes an annual membership resource directory and a newsletter.

15. **Association for Women in Computing,** 41 Sutter Street, Suite 1006, San Francisco, CA 94104, (415) 905-4663, Fax (415) 391-1709, **http://www.awc-hq.org/awc** - AWC is a non-profit organization dedicated to the professional development and advancement of women in computing. The organization publishes a newsletter, *National Newsbytes,* ten times per year.

16. **Association for Women in Mathematics,** 4114 Computer and Space Sciences Building, University of Maryland, College Park, MD 10742-2461, (301) 405-7892, **http://www.awm-math.org/** - AWM encourages equal opportunity for women in the mathematical sciences. *The AWM Newsletter* is published bi-monthly.

17. **Association for Women in Psychology,** L. Gallahan College of Arts & Science, Pacific University, 2043 College Way, Forest Grove, OR 97116, (503) 359-2216 - AWP is a non-profit scientific and educational feminist organization. Members are devoted to evaluating the role psychology and mental health play in women's lives. AWP publishes a quarterly newsletter.

18. **Association for Women in Science,** 1200 New York Avenue, Suite 650, Washington, DC 20005, (202) 326-8940, Fax (202) 326-8960, **http://www.awis.org** - AWIS is a non-profit organization dedicated to increasing the opportunities of women in all fields of science. AWIS publishes a bi-monthly magazine, *AWIS Magazine.*

19. **Association for Women Lawyers,** 260 E. Highland Avenue, Suite 700, Milwaukee, WI 53202, (414) 225-0260, Fax (414) 225-9666 - AWL is a member bar association of lawyers, judges and law students from all areas of practice and levels of expertise. AWL publishes a monthly newsletter.

20. **Association of Real Estate Women,** 250 West 57th Street, Suite 2301, New York, NY 10107, (212) 265-4652, Fax (212) 265-4974 - AREW membership is drawn from the real estate industry including: bankers, brokers, property managers, construction executives, attorneys, architects, and marketing.

21. **Association of Women's Music and Culture,** 2124 Kittredge Street, #104, Berkeley, CA 94705, (541) 484-6140, **http://www.connix.com/~psmith/awmac** - A feminist professional organization engaged in the enhancement of women's music and culture.

22. **Business and Professional Women/USA,** 2012 Massachusetts Avenue, NW, Washington, DC 20036, (202) 293-1100, Fax (202) 861-0298, http://www.bpwusa.org/ - BPW/USA with its non-profit Foundation, is one of the largest and oldest women's professional organizations in the world. BPW//USA promotes equity for all women in the workplace through advocacy, education and information. *National Business Woman Magazine* is their quarterly magazine.

23. **Business Women's Network,** 1146 Nineteenth Street, NW, Third Floor, Washington, DC 20036, (800) 48-WOMEN, Fax (202) 833-1808, **http://www.businesswomensnetwork.com/** - BWN encourages communication and networking between the top businesswomen's organization in the

United States. BWN publishes a comprehensive directory of over 6,000 women's organizations and websites. BWN publishes a bi-monthly newsletter titled *Update*.

24. **Catalyst,** 250 Park Avenue South, New York, NY 10003-1459, (212) 777-8900, Fax (212) 514-7600, **http://www.catalystwomen.org** - A nonprofit organization focusing the attention of business leaders and public-policy makers on women's leadership development and woman issues. *Perspective* is the monthly newsletter.

25. **Center For The American Woman and Politics,** Eagleton Institute of Politics, Rutgers University, New Brunswick, NJ 08901 (732) 932-9384, Fax (732) 932-6778, **http://www.rcl.rutgers.edu/~cawp/** - CAWP is a university-based research, education and public service center. Its mission is to promote greater understanding and knowledge about women's relationship to politics and government and to enhance women's influence and leadership in public life. CAWP is a unit of *Eagleton Institute of Politics at Rutgers, The State University of New Jersey*.

26. **Coalition of Labor Union Women,** 1126 16th Street, NW, Washington, DC 20036, (202) 466-4610/4615, Fax (202) 776-0537 - CLUW has led the fight for the rights of working women. CLUW News is the bi-monthly member newsletter.

27. **Committee of 200,** 625 North Michigan Avenue, Suite 500, Chicago, IL 60611-3108, (312) 751-3477, Fax (312) 943-9401 - C200 is the premiere professional organization of prominent businesswomen who personify the spirit of entrepreneurs, business and leadership. It is an international organization with 375 members, divided into four U.S. regions including an international segment. C200 produces a monthly newsletter *Network*.

28. **Emily's List,** 805 15th Street, NW, Suite 400, Washington, DC 20005, (202) 326-1400, Fax (202) 326-1415, **http://www.emilyslist.org/** - Emily's List is a political network for pro-choice democratic women.

29. **Fashion Group, The,** 597 Fifth Avenue, New York, NY 10017, (212) 593-1715, Fax (212) 593-1925, **http://www.fgi.org** - The Fashion Group International is a global non-profit association of women of achievement and influence representing all areas of the fashion and related industries.

30. **Federally Employed Women,** 1400 Eye Street, NW, Suite 425, Washington, DC 20005-2252, (202) 898-0994, Fax (202) 898-0998, **http://www.few.org** - FEW was organized as a non-profit membership association to eliminate sex discrimination and sexual harassment and to enhance career opportunities for women in government. FEW's *News and Views* is a bi-monthly newspaper.

31. **Feminist Majority Foundation, The,** Feminist Career Center, 1600 Wilson Blvd., Suite 801, Arlington, VA 22209, (703) 522-2214, Fax (703) 522-2219, **http://www.feminist.org/911/911jobs.html** - FMF works to win more representation in Congress and state and local elective government by launching a nation-wide campaign to recruit more women to run for political office. FMF publishes a periodic journal called the *Feminist Majority Report.*

32. **Financial Women International,** 200 North Glebe Road, Suite 814, Arlington, VA 22203-3728, (703) 807-2007, Fax (703) 807-0111, **http://www.fwi.org** - FWI's mission is to network women in all sectors of the financial services industry. *Financial Woman Today* is published six times annually.

33. **General Federation of Women's Clubs,** 1734 N Street, NW, Washington, DC 20036-2990, (202) 347-3168, (800) 443-GFWC Fax (202) 835-0246 - The GFWC members are united by a dedicated to community improvement through volunteer services. Provides several publications throughout the year.

34. **Home-Based Working Moms,** P.O. Box 500164, Austin, TX 78750, (512) 918-0670, **http://www.hbwm.com** - HBWM is a national organization founded to provide support and information to start a work-at-home career or to help make their current home career more successful. There is a monthly newsletter.

35. **Institute for Research on Women's Health,** 1825 I Street, NW, Suite 400 Washington, DC 20006, (301) 564-0184, (202) 483-8643 Fax (301) 564-0987 - IRWH is dedicated to research, education and policy work related to the health and mental health of women and minorities and the advancement of scientific and scholarly work.

36. **International Alliance, The,** P.O. Box 1119 Sparks-Glencoe, Baltimore, MD 21152-1119, (410) 472-4221, Fax (410) 472-2920, **http://www.t-i-a.com** - TIA is an organization dedicated to promoting qualified women into decision-making positions in government, business and civic affairs. Network membership is open to statewide, local or corporate networks of executives and professional women. *The Alliance* is the bi-monthly newsletter.

37. **International Association of Administrative Professionals,** 10502 NW Ambassador Dr., Kansas City, MO 64195-0404, (816) 891-6600, Fax (816) 891-9119, **http://www.iaap.org** - IAAP represents administrative staff in fifty-seven nations. IAAP nationally and internationally provides resources and strategies for administrative personnel.

38. **International Association for Feminist Economics,** c/o Jean Shackelford, Dept. Of Economics, Bucknell University, Lewisburg, PA 17837, (717) 524-3441 Fax (717) 524-3451 - IAFFE is a non-profit organization advancing feminist inquiry of economic issues and educating economists and others on feminist points of view on economic issues. Publishes a journal, *Feminist Economics* and a newsletter.

39. **International Aviation Women's Association,** 1251 Avenue of the Americas, New York, NY 10020, (212) 894-6700, Fax (212) 575-1297 - IAWA is an organization for women who are senior aviation defense attorney's, executives and managers in the aviation insurance industry, the aerospace manufacturing industry, airlines, and related governmental agencies. IAWA publishes a quarterly newsletter.

40. **International Women's Forum,** 1621 Connecticut NW, #300, Washington, DC 20009, (202) 775-8917 Fax (202) 429-0271 - IWF members provide a network of support and help prepare future generations of women leaders through its Leadership Foundation. Publishes an annual membership directory and a quarterly newsletter, *The Connection.*

41. **International Women's Media Foundation,** 1726 M Street, NW #1002, Washington, DC 20036, (202) 496-1992 Fax (202) 496-1977 - IWMF's mission is to strengthen the role of women in the media worldwide. It works to provide coordinated, comprehensive resource sharing and professional support. Publishes a quarterly newsletter, *IWMF Wire* and the annual *IWMF Network Directory.*

42. **International Women's Writing Guild,** P.O. Box 810, Gracie Station, New York, NY 10028 (212) 737-7536 Fax (212) 737-9469 - IWWG members are a widely diverse group of women representing all nationalities, colors, creeds, ages and occupations who network for the personal and professional empowerment of women through writing. A portfolio is not required for membership. Publishes a bi-monthly newsletter, *Network.*

43. **League of Women Voters,** 1730 M Street, NW, Washington, DC 20036, (202) 429-1965 (800) 249-VOTE, Fax (202) 429-0854, **http://www.electriciti.com/%7Elwvus/index.html** - LWV is a multi-issue, non-partisan organization, encouraging the active participation of citizens in government. *The National Voter* magazine is available to members.

44. **National Association for Female Executives,** 135 West 50th Street, 16th Floor, New York, NY 10020, (212) 445-6235, Fax (212) 445-6228, **http://www.nafe.com** - NAFE provides resources and strategies for professional women. *Executive Female* is the monthly magazine.

45. **National Association for Girls and Women in Sports,** 1900 Association Drive, Reston, VA 20191, (703) 476-3452, Fax (703) 476-9527 - NAGWS is an educational organization dedicated to developing and promoting women for sport leadership positions. NAGWS publishes the *GWS News*, a five-times-a-year journal.

46. **National Association for Women in Education,** 1325 18th Street, NW, Suite 210, Washington, DC 20036, (202) 659-9330, Fax (202) 457-0946 - NAWE is a national professional organization providing support to women educators. *About Women on Campus* is the quarterly newsletter.

47. **National Association of Home Builders Women's Council,** 1201 15th Street NW, Washington, DC 20005-2800, (202) 822-0433/(800) 368-5242 Ext. 433, Fax (202) 861-2170, **http://www.nahb.com** - NAHB Women's Council supports the professional development of women in the home-building industry. The Council publishes a bi-monthly newsletter called *Networker*.

48. **National Association of Insurance Women,** 1847 East 15th Street, Tulsa, OK 74104, (918) 744-5195, Fax (918) 743-1968, **http://www.naiw.org** - NAIW promotes the education and advancement of women employed in the insurance industry. *Today's Insurance Women* is NAIW's bi-monthly magazine. *Leadership News* is the bi-monthly newsletter.

49. **National Association of Women Artists,** 41 Union Square West, Room 906, New York, NY 10003-3278, (212) 675-1616 - NAWA is a non-profit, member supported, national art association for women in the fine arts. NAWA publishes a catalogue listing members and award winners and two newsletters per year.

50. **National Association of Women Business Owners,** 1100 Wayne Avenue, Suite 830, Silver Springs, MD 20910, (301) 608-2590, Fax (301) 608-2596, **http://www.nawbo.org** - NAWBO networks women business owners to expand opportunities for women in business. NAWBO publishes a national magazine *Enterprising Women*.

51. **National Association of Women in Construction,** 327 South Adams Street, Fort Worth, TX 76108, (817) 877-5551, Fax (817) 877-0324, **http://www.nawic.org** - NAWIC is an international organization that promotes and supports the advancement of women within the construction industry. NAWIC publishes a monthly magazine *The NAWIC Image*.

52. **National Association of Women's Business Advocates,** 100 West Randolph, Suite 3-400, Chicago, IL 60067, (312) 814-7176, Fax (312) 814-5247, **http://www.nawba.org** - A national organization serving as an advocate for women business owners by fostering a nationwide awareness of the economic contribution made by this growing business segment. NAWBA publishes a quarterly newsletter entitled *NAWBA Notes*. The Representative is the State Woman Business Advocate or representative appointed by the governor.

Appendix

53. **National Association of Working Women, 9 to 5,** 238 West Wisconsin. #900, Milwaukee, WI 53203, (414) 274-0925, Fax (414) 272-2870 - 9 to 5 is a membership and advocacy organization devoted to improve the pay and status of working women with a primary focus on women office workers. The 9to5 *Newsline* is published five times a year.

54. **National Conference of State Legislatures - Women's Network,** 1560 Broadway, Suite 700, Denver, CO 80202, (303) 830-2200, Fax (303) 863-8003 - The Women's Network's purpose is to develop, strengthen and support participation, leadership and partnerships among women legislators within National Conference of State Legislatures (NCSL) and their own states. *Network News* is published three times yearly.

55. **National Foundation for Women Legislators,** 910 16th Street, NW, Suite 100, Washington, DC 20006, (202) 337-3565, Fax (202) 337-3566, **http:// www.womenlegislators.org** - The foundation's mission is to provide strategic resources for women to be strong and effective state legislators.

56. **National Museum of Women in the Arts,** New York Avenue and 13th Street, NW, Washington, DC 20034, (202) 783-5000, **http:// www.nmwa.org** - The National Museum of Women in the Arts brings recognition to the achievements of women artists of all periods and nationalities by exhibiting, preserving, acquiring and researching art by women and by educating the public concerning their accomplishments.

57. **National Organization for Women,** 1000 16th Street NW, Suite 700, Washington, DC 20036, (202) 331-0066, Fax (202) 785-8576, **http:// www.now.org** - NOW's goal is to develop action plans fostering equality for all women. NOW publishes the bi-monthly magazine *National NOW Times.*

58. **National Women's History Project, The,** 7738 Bell Road, Windsor, CA 95492, (707) 838-6000, Fax (707) 838-0478 - NWHP is a non-profit educational organization whose mission is to "write women back into history". The organization initiated National Women's History Month, now observed coast to coast each March. Multiple resources and seminars are available. *Network News* is the quarterly, eight-page newsletter.

59. **National Women's Political Caucus, The,** 1630 Connecticut Avenue, NW, Suite 425, Washington, DC 20009, (202) 785-1100, Fax (202) 785-3605, **http://www.feminist.com/nwpc.htm** - NWPC is a national grassroots, organization dedicated to increasing the number of women in elected and appointed office at all levels of government, regardless of party affiliation. *The Women's Political Times* is NWPC's quarterly newsletter.

60. **Network of Women in Computer Technology,** P.O. Box 59504, Philadelphia, PA 19102-9504, (215) 934-3600 - NWCT is a non-profit organization dedicated to enhancing the careers of their members who are professionals in information systems. NWCT publishes a monthly newsletter.

61. **Organization of Women in International Trade,** P.O. Box 65962, Washington, DC 20035, (202) 628-2446, Fax (202) 785-9842, http://www.owit.org - OWIT is a non-profit corporation promoting the interest of women in the field of international trade.

62. **Professional Women Controllers, Inc.,** P.O. Box 44085, Oklahoma City, OK 73144, (800) 232-9PWC - PWC is a non-profit, professional air traffic controllers association. Members consist of all levels of employees, from Air Traffic Assistants to members of the Senior Executive Service. *The WATCH* is the national quarterly newsletter.

63. **Roundtable for Women in Foodservice, Inc.,** 1372 LaColina Drive, Tustin, CA 92780, (800) 898-2849 or (714) 838-2749, Fax (714) 838-2750 - RWF's goal is to help women progress and succeed in the foodservice industry. The *Annual Pacesetter Journal* is a national quarterly newsletter.

64. **Section for Women in Public Administration,** American Society for Public Administration, 1120 G Street, NW, Washington, DC 20005, (202) 393-7878, Fax (202) 638-4952 - SWPA develops programs and projects that promote the full participation of women in all levels and areas of the public sector. SWPA publishes a newsletter *Bridging the Gap.*

65. **Society of Women Engineers, The,** 120 Wall Street, Eleventh Floor, New York, NY 10005-3902, (212) 509-9577, Fax (212) 509-0224, http://www.swe.org - SWE's mission is to advocate for women to achieve full potential in careers as engineers and leaders. SWE publishes a newsletter entitled *AWE Magazine.*

66. **Soroptimist International of the Americas,** 2 Penn Center Plaza, Suite 1000, Philadelphia, PA 19102-1883, (215) 557-9300, Fax (215) 568-5200, http://www.siahq.com - SIA was founded in 1921 as a service organization to improve society with special attention to women. A magazine is published six times a year.

67. **Tradeswomen, Inc.,** P.O. Box 2622, Berkeley, CA 94710, (510) 433-1378, Fax (510) 649-6277 - A national, non-profit membership organization offering peer support, networking and advocacy for women in non-traditional, blue-collar jobs. *Tradeswomen Magazine* is the national publication.

68. **Webgrrls,** 50 Broad Street, Suite 1614, New York, NY 10004, (212) 642-8012, http://www.webgrrls.com - Webgrrls is a real-world face-to-face networking group for women working in and interested in web marketing and design.

69. **Wider Opportunities for Women,** 815 15th Street, NW, Suite 916, Washington, DC 20005, (202) 638-3143, Fax (202) 638-4885 - WOW works nationally to achieve economic independence and equality of opportunity for women and girls. The newsletter is *Women at Work.*

70. **Women as Allies,** P.O. Box 794, Boulder Creek, CA 95006, (408) 338-3637, Fax (408) 338-0843, http://www.Women-As-Allies.org - A multiracial, multicultural organization dedicated to women mentoring women. National and international presentations are held to facilitate women with decision-making power being inclusive with other women.

71. **Women Chefs & Restauranteurs,** 304 W. Liberty Street, #201, Louisville, KY 40202, (415) 362-7336, Fax (415) 362-7335 - WCR promotes the education and advancement of women in the restaurant industry. WCR publishes a quarterly newsletter.

72. **Women Employed/Women Employed Institute,** 22 West Monroe, Suite 1400, Chicago, IL 60603, (312) 782-3902, Fax (312) 782-5249 - WE/WEI empowers women to improve their economic status through advocacy, direct service and public education. WEI has published guides, studies and directories on issues affecting working women.

73. **Women Health Executives Network,** P.O. Box 350, Kenilworth, IL 60043-0350, (847) 251-1400, Fax (847) 256-5601 - WHEN members represent, provide and support the delivery of health services.

74. **Women Incorporated,** 333 South Grand Avenue, #2450, Los Angeles, CA 90071, (213) 680-3375, (800) 930-3993, Fax (213) 680-3475, Organization's goal is to improve the economic power of women entrepreneurs through advocacy, technical assistance, and funding resources.

75. **Women in Aerospace,** P.O. Box 16721, Alexandria, VA 22302, (202) 547-9451, **http://www.anser.org/wia** - WIA is dedicated to expanding women's opportunities for leadership and increasing its visibility in the aerospace community. WIA membership receives monthly newsletters.

76. **Women in Aviation International,** 3647 S.R. 503 South, West Alexandria, Ohio 45381, (937) 839-4647, Fax (937) 839-4645, **http://www.wiai.org/wia** - WIAI was formed to encourage women to explore aviation careers. Bimonthly magazine is published.

77. **Women in Cable & Telecommunications,** 230 West Monroe, Suite 730, Chicago, IL 60606, (312) 634-2330, Fax (312) 634-2345, **http://www.wict.org** - WICT focuses on issues related to the empowerment of women and workforce productivity. *The Source* is a bi-monthly newsletter that is published.

78. **Women in Community Service,** 1900 North Beauregard Street, Suite 103, Alexandria, VA 22311, (703) 671-0500, Fax (703) 671-4489 - WICS is an independent, non-profit corporation dedicated to creating and identifying employment opportunities and training individuals in need of these jobs. WICS publishes *The WICS Magazine* quarterly.

79. **Women in Engineering Program Advocates Network,** WEPAN Member Services, 1284 CIVL Building, Room G167, West Lafayette, IN 47907-1284, (765) 494-5387, Fax (765) 494-9152, **http://www.engr.washington.edu/~wepan/** - WEPAN is a non-profit organization founded to effect a positive change in the engineering infrastructure. The academic and social climate become conducive to women in engineering. WEPAN publishes *EPANEWS*.

80. **Women in Film,** 6464 Sunset Boulevard #1080, Hollywood, CA 90028, (213) 463-6040, Fax (213) 463-0963 - WIF is a non-profit organization for women in the global communications industry. WIF publishes a monthly newsletter entitled *REEL NEWS*.

81. **Women in Management,** 30 North Michigan Avenue, Suite 508, Chicago, IL 60602-3404, (312) 263-3636, Fax (312) 372-8738 - WIM provides networking, professional development, and educational opportunities for women in management and leadership positions.

82. **Women in Military Service For America,** Department 560, Washington, DC 20042-0560, (703) 533-1155, (800) 222-2294, Fax (703) 931-4208, **http://www.wimsa.org/pub/wimsa/home.html** - A national organization that links women who have served in the military or are currently serving. They also recognize women who participated in the national defense, such as the Red Cross or USO. WMSFA publishes a newsletter three times a year and *The Register*.

83. **Women in Packaging, Inc.,** 4290 Bells Ferry Road, Suite 106-17, Kennesaw, GA 30144, (770) 924-3563, Fax (770) 928-2338, **http://www.fdp.com/womeninpackaging** - A non-profit organization dedicated to eliminating stereotypes and discrimination against women in packaging. The newsletter, *Update*, is published on a bi-monthly basis.

84. **Women in Technology International,** 4641 Burnet Avenue, Sherman Oaks, CA 91403, (800) 334-WITI, Fax (818) 906-3299, **http://www.witi.com** - WITI members represent a cross sector of women working in science and technology organizations. WITI has established a Hall of Fame to recognize the accomplishments of women.

85. **Women in the Fire Service,** P.O. Box 5446, Madison, WI 53705, (608) 233-4768, Fax (608) 233-4879 - WFS membership is open to all who are interested in seeing a smooth transition to a gender-integrated fire service work force. *Firework* is a monthly newsletter that WFS publishes.

86. **Women Legislator's Lobby,** 110 Maryland Avenue, NE, Suite 205, Washington, DC 20002, (202) 543-8505, Fax (202) 675-6469 - A bipartisan organization of women state legislators working to influence the formulation of federal laws, policies, and budget priorities.

87. **Women's Council of Realtors,** 430 North Michigan Avenue, Chicago, IL 60611, (312) 329-8483, Fax (312) 329-3290, **http://www.wcr.org** - WCR is a community of real estate professionals dedicated to serving members by providing opportunities for personal and career growth. *Communique* is the official magazine published by WCR eight times a year.

88. **Women's Environment & Development Organization,** 355 Lexington Avenue, 3rd Floor, New York, NY 10017-6603, (212) 973-0325, Fax (212) 973-0335, **http://www.wedo.org** - The organization aims to promote women playing major roles in the growing worldwide movement for global security, economic justice, democracy, human rights and women's empowerment.

89. **Women's Fisheries Network,** 2442 NW Market Street, #243, Seattle, WA 98107, (206) 789-1987, Fax (206) 789-1987, **http://web.mit.edu/ seagrant/www/wfn.html** - WFN provides a forum for timely and sometimes controversial issues which affect the fishing and related industries. A regular newsletter is published.

90. **Women's Foreign Policy Group,** 1875 Connecticut Avenue, NW, Suite 720, Washington, DC 20009-5728, (202) 884-8597, Fax (202) 884-8499 - WFPG is a non-profit, educational organization dedicated to global engagement and the promotion of the leadership of women in international affairs professions.

91. **Women's Franchise Network, http://www.franchise.org/wfn/** - WFN is an international networking forum for those entering the franchise world and those established in the field. Publications are *IFA Insider* and *Franchising World Magazine.*

92. **Women's Information Network,** 1800 R St., NW Unit C-4, Washington, DC 20009, (202) 347-2827, Fax (202) 347-1418, **http:// www.winonline.org** - WIN was founded to create a social, professional and political support system needed for career women looking for jobs or changing careers. *The Winning State* is WIN's monthly newsletter.

93. **Women's International Center,** P.O. Box 880736, San Diego, CA 92108, (619) 295-6446, Fax (619) 296-1633, **http://www.wic.org** - WIC acknowledges, honors, encourages and educates women everywhere. *Communique,* a quarterly newsletter is published for members.

94. **Women's International Network of Utility Professionals,** P.O. Box 335, Whites Creek, TN 37189, (615) 876-5444, Fax (615) 876-5444 - EWRT is a professional association that benefits the electric industry and allied fields. *The Pulse* and *The Connection* are a member newsletters.

95. **Women's Jewelry Association, The**, 333B Route 46 West, Suite B-201, Fairfield, NJ 07004, (973) 575-7190, Fax (201) 575-1445 - Organization created to help executive women in the industry to advance. A bi-annual newsletter is published.

96. **Women's Pro Rodeo Association,** 1235 Lake Plaza, Suite 134, Colorado Springs, CO 80906, (719) 576-0900, Fax (719) 576-1386 - Organizes and promotes women in the sport of professional rodeo. The monthly newsletter published is *WPRA News.*

97. **Women's Research and Education Institute,** 1750 New York Ave, NW, Suite 350, Washington, DC 20006, (202) 628-0444, **http://www.wrei.org** - WREI is an independent, non-profit non-partisan organization committed to equity for women and their roles in the family, workplace, and public arena. WREI provides research information to help shape public policy.

98. **Women's Transportation Seminar,** One Walnut Street, Boston, MA 02108, (617) 367-3273, Fax (617) 227-6783, **http://www.wtsnational.org** - WTS is a national organization of transportation professions. WTS members work in many different transportation modes such as aviation, public transportation, rail, highways and maritime. WTS publishes a bi-monthly national newsletter.

99. **Women's World Banking,** 8 West 40th Street, New York, NY 10018, (212) 719-0414 - WWB is a global non-profit financial institution advancing and promoting the full economic participation of women. *What Works* is WWB's newsletter, published in English, Spanish and French.

100. **Zonta International,** 557 West Randolph Street, Chicago, IL 60661, (312) 930-5848, Fax (312) 930-0951 - Zonta International's mission is to advance the status of women worldwide. Zonta works with United Nation agencies to implement service projects to benefit women. Zonta is located in sixty-nine countries. *The Zontian* is the organization's official quarterly publication.

Websites for selected organizations are included in their descriptions.

1. Advancing Women
http://www.advancingwomen.com
Bilingual website offering business and technology news, journal for woman researchers and educators, and career strategies for women in the workplace.

2. Amazon City
http://www.amazoncity.com
Comprehensive site listing businesses you can browse, a community of information with the Amazon City Café, discussion areas, mailing lists, and an informational hotspot in the form of libraries, zines, museums, and everything else you'd get in a big city.

3. Angel Swan's World of Women's Resources
http://www.nr.infi.net/~drmatrix/wstart.htm
ASWWR offers an alphabetical listing of organizations, and resources for all kinds of women. The site also connects to an on-line Survey of Women with facts and statistics on women and the web.

4. Best Companies for Working Mothers
http://www.womenswire.com/work
One hundred companies are profiled on benefits provided for working Mothers.

5. BizWomen
http://www.bizwomen.com
Site provides an on-line interactive marketplace to communicate, network, exchange ideas and provide support for each other. In process of merging with Field of Dreams.

6. CareerBabe
http://www.careerbabe.com
An on-line job search resource for women and resource for Internet career sites.

7. Cyber SpaceGirls
http://www.swflbisnet.com/cybergal.htm
Provides women with business advice and guidance. Assists women with small businesses, law, physics, and technology interests.

8. Digital Women
http://www.digital-women.com
Provides resources for women in business, businesswomen, women who own their own business and women with home-based businesses. International resource for women to find anything they need for their businesses.

9. Electra Pages, The
http://www.electrapages.com
Website consisting of 7,000 women's organizations and businesses. You are able to search by alphabetical listing, type of organization, or geographic location. Mailing lists can also be ordered.

10. Equal Rights Advocates
http://www.equalrights.org
ERA is one of the oldest and respected women's law centers in the nation. This site provides for the advancement of women through establishment of their economic, social, and political equality.

11. Fabulous Net Women
http://www.interport.net/~dolphin/netwomen.html
Website that lists unique sites and provides detailed information about women on the Internet, women's organizations and other resources.

12. Femina
http://www.femina.com
Provides women with a comprehensive, searchable directory of links to female-friendly sites and information on the World Wide Web.

13. Feminist Activist Resources on the Net
http://www.igc.apc.org/women/feminist.html
Comprehensive listing of topics related to feminism, women's studies, and general women's issues.

14. Feminist.com
http://www.feminist.com
Comprehensive site offering women quotes, weekly updates, bookstore, nationwide database of thousands of women's resources and more. Goal of the site is to make networking easier for women and to create a women's cyber community.

15. Feminist Internet Gateway, The
http://www.feminist.org/gateway/ru486one.html
Comprehensive list of links to sites that promote women's interests.

16. Field of Dreams
http://www.fodreams.com
A networking source for women in business. Forums, discussions, information, and resources are available.

17. Glass Ceiling, The
http://www.theglassceiling.com
Presents information to women in order to keep them up-to-date with events and news concerning women obtaining upper-level positions.

18. Herspace Network
http://www.herspace.com

A group of diverse sites by and for women. excellent resources available on business, parenting, and life. Each unique site shares the common goal of supporting the success of women.

19. Institute for Women's Policy Research, The
http://www.iwpr.org

IWPR is a non-profit, independent, scientific research organization. The goal is to inform and stimulate debate on issues of critical importance.

20. International Women's Writing Guild
http://www.iwwg.com

IWWG is a network for the personal and professional empowerment of women through writing.

21. Leadership America
http://www.leadershipamerica.com

Organization dedicated to connecting outstanding women and providing professional development programs.

22. New Women: New Leadership
http://www.newleadership.com

Multi-media project about women as leaders and how the leadership process works.

23. Small Business Association, Office of Women's Bureau Ownership
http://www.sbaonline.sba.gov/womeninbusiness

SBA's OWBO has 70 women's business centers in 40 states plus the internet center. OWBO conducts mentoring roundtables and helps women start and build successful businesses.

24. University of Maryland Women's Studies Database
http://www.inform.umd.edu/WMST

Information packed site on general women's issues and the women's studies profession.

25. Virtual Sisterhood
http://www.igc.apc.org/vsister/vsister.html

Dedicated to enhancing women's activism through effective use of electronic communications. Priority's to include immigrant and refugee women and low-income women in the electronic age.

26. Voices of Women
http://www.systers.org

Site offers articles on a wide variety of topics, calendar of events, bridges to other destinations on the Web, a directory of woman-friendly businesses and a marketplace.

27. Washington Feminist, Faxnet (WFF)
http://www.feminist.com/ffn.htm
Initiative of the non-profit Center for Advancement of Public Policy to
mobilize women to advocate for their legal, social, and economic rights. WFF
is underwritten by feminist organizations, allowing a weekly two-page
newsletter to be, Faxed for a nominal charge.

28. WomanOwned
http://www.womanowned.com
Provides women in business networking opportunities and business
information to assist in achieving success.

29. Women Business Owners Corporation, The
http://www.wboc.org/framedoc/mainbody.html
WBOC network provides electronic access to corporate and government
contracts.

30. Women Executives in State Government (WESG)
http://www.wesg.org
National non-profit organization committed to excellence in state
government and the development of future leaders.

31. Women for Healthcare Education, Reform and Equity (WHERE)
http://www.med.com/where
A national non-profit organization dedicated to educating and supporting
women on healthcare issues.

32. Women Leaders Online/Woman Organizing For Change
http://www.w/o.org
WLO/WOC is a woman's advocacy group organizing non-partisan, grassroots
lobbying and encouraging pro-woman candidates. Action Alerts and
interactive discussions are available.

33. Women of Wisdom
http://www.womenofwisdom.com
Advocates for women to increase their comfort with the utilization of power. Offers
networking, books, gift items, executive coaching, speaker services and seminars.

34. Women on Wallstreet
http://www.womenonwallstreet.com
A businesswomen's association providing resources and services through the
World Wide Web, linking women and empowering its members to achieve
their career success and financial security.

35. Women@Work
http://www.nafe.com
A business network guide to resources for working women.

36. Women's Bureau Clearinghouse, The
http://www.dol.gov/dol/wb/public/programs/house.htm
Sponsored by the Women's Bureau, Department of Labor, the Clearinghouse is a computerized database and resource center responsive to women's workplace issues. The workforce quality issues include information on the rights of women workers and the agencies that enforce these rights.

37. Women's Connection On-line
http://www.womenconnect.com
WCO offers extensive services through bulletin board discussions, live chats, and a directory of women business owners. WCO offers links to over fifty websites that are useful to women in business.

38. Women's Cybrary
http://www.womenbooks.com
Website offers organizations and societies supporting women's writing.

39. Women's Institute for Freedom of the Press
http://www.igc.org/wifp
WIFP's goal is to increase communication among women, primarily media women and media-concerned women.

40. Women's Internet Council
http://www.rain.org/wic.html
WIC is a link to various business topics and areas of interest to women.

41. Women's Media
http://www.womensmedia.com
Self-help site for women with multiple features.

42. Women's National Book Association
http://www.he.net/~susannah/wnba.htm
Website connecting all occupations in the publishing industry.

43. Women's Online Community Network
http://www.womenbusiness.com
Site offering advertisements for your business, chatting with other women in business and finding business resources and tools you need.

44. Women's Resource & Yellow Pages
http://www.workingwoman.com
A complete directory of women-owned businesses, professional services and community services for women.

45. Women's Resource Project, The
http://www.sunsite.unc.edu/cheryb/women
Resource for women's topics including academics, organizations and publications.

46. Women's Wire
http://www.women.com
This is an on-line magazine featuring world, health and fashion news for women and questions and answers for a variety of forums.

47. Women's Work
http://www.wwork.com
Website offers you articles, forums, and chats hosted by today's top business experts, interviews of successful business professionals, a wide array of tele-workshops to help you on the job and chat rooms.

48. WomenZone
http://www.womenzone.com
Features articles and discussions that relate to the lives of today's career woman including, a forum for women in business.

49. WoRDWeb; the: Women's Resource Directory
http://www.ghgcorp.com/wordweb
Site is an annual on-line professional directory of women in business that presents classified listings and advertisements of women-owned businesses and professional women.

50. WWWomen
http://www.wwwomen.com
Site dedicated to finding all sites on the Internet relevant to women.

Resources & Bibliography

Chapter 1

Aburdene, Patricia, Naisbitt, John. (1992). *Megatrends for Women: From Liberation to Leadership.* New York, NY: Ballantine Books, 24.

Benson, Herbert, Stuart, Eileen M. (1992). *The Wellness Book: The Comprehensive Guide to Maintaining Health and Treating Stress-Related Illness.* Secaucus, NJ: Carol Publishing.

Costello, Cynthia B., Miles, Shari, & Stone, Anne J. (eds.) (1998). *The American Woman 1999-2000.* New York, NY: W.W. Norton & Co., Inc.

Cummings, Nicholas A. (May 1985). *Saving Health Care Dollars through Psychological Service.*

Davidson, Marilyn J., & Cooper, Cary L. (1992). *Shattering the Glass Ceiling: The Woman Manager.* London: Paul Chapman Publishing Ltd.

Del Valle, Christina. (October 24, 1994). "Glass Ceiling? What Glass Ceiling?" *Businessweek.*

Denmark, Florence L. (1993). "Women, Leadership, and Empowerment." *Psychology of Women Quarterly,* 17:343-356.

Epstein, Gene. (December 1, 1997). "Low Ceiling: How women are held back by sexism at work and child-rearing duties at home." *Barron's Periodical,* 35-40.

Friedan, Betty. (1963). *The Feminine Mystique.* New York, NY: W.W. Norton & Co., Inc.

Gaskill, Stephen. (November 1995). "A Solid Investment: Making Full Use of the Nations' Human Capital." *Recommendations of the Federal Glass Ceiling Commission.* Washington, D.C.: U.S. Government Printing Office.

Goss, Tracy. (1996). *The Last Word on Power: Executive Re-Invention for Leaders Who Must Make the Impossible Happen.* New York, NY: Doubleday, 15.

Griscom, Joan L. (1992). "Women and Power: Definition, Dualism, and Difference." *Psychology of Women Quarterly,* 16, 389-414.

Heim, Pat, Golant, Susan K. (1992). *Hardball for Women.* Los Angeles, CA: Penguin Books.

Horner, Althea J. (1989). *The Wish for Power and the Fear of Having It.* Northvale, NJ: Jason Aronson, Inc.

Jenkins, Sharon Rae. (1994). "Need for Power and Women's Careers Over 14 Years." *Journal of Personality and Social Psychology*, 66:1, 155-165

Lips, Hilary, M. (1991). *Women, Men, and Power.* Mountain View, CA: Mayfield Publishing Co.

Martz, Sandra Haldeman. (1998). *at our core.*: Women Writing About Power. Watsonville, CA: Papier-Mache Press.

McGrath, Ellen, Keita, Gwendoyn Puryear, Strickland, Bonnie R., Russo, Nancy Felipe (ed.). (1990). *Women and Depression.* Washington, D.C.: American Psychological Association.

Melia, Jinx. (1986). *Breaking into the Boardroom*: What Every Woman Needs to Know. New York, NY: G.P. Putnam's Sons.

Mendell, Adrienne. (1996). *How Men Think: The Seven Essential Rules for Making It in a Man's World.* New York, NY: Fawcett Columbine Books.

Miller, Cynthia L. & Cummins, A.Gaye. (1992). "An Examination of Women's Perspectives on Power." *Psychology of Women Quarterly*, 16:4, 415-428.

Offermann, Lyn R., & Beil, Cheryl. (1992). "Achievement Styles of Women Leaders and their Peers." *Psychology of Women Quarterly*, 16:1, 53.

Offerman, Lyn R. (1986). "The Development and Validation of The Power Apprehension Scale." *Educational and Psychological Measurement*, 46, 437-441.

Prokop, Charles K., & Bradley, Laurence A. (ed.). (1981). *Medical Psychology*, New York, NY: Academic Press.

Reid-Merritt, Patricia. (1996). *Sister Power: How Phenomenal Black Women Are Rising to the Top.* New York, NY: John Wiley & Sons, Inc., 192.

Rubin, Harriet. (1997). The PRINCESSA: Machiavelli for Women. New York, NY: Bantam Doubleday Dell Publishing Group, Inc., 21.

Warner, Carolyn. (1992). *The Last Word.* Englewood Cliffs, NJ: Prentice Hall, 177.

Webster's New Universal Unabridged Dictionary. (1996). New York, NY: Random House Value Publishing Inc., 1516.

Wolf, Naomi. (1993). *Fire with Fire: The New Female Power and How To Use It.* New York, NY: Random House, Inc., preface.

Yoder, Janice D., & Kahn, Arnold S. (1992). "Toward a Feminist Understanding of Women and Power." *Psychology of Women Quarterly*, 16:4, 381-388.

Chapter 2

Baruch, Grace K. (1988). *Reflections on Guilt, Women, and Gender.* Wellesley College, Center for Research on Women, Working Papers Series 176.

Bem, Sandra Lipsitz. (1993). *The Lenses of Gender: Transforming the Debate on Sexual Inequality.* New Haven, Connecticut: Yale University Press.

Benson, Herbert, Stuart, Eileen M. (1992). *The Wellness Book: The Comprehensive Guide to Maintaining Health and Treating Stress-Related Illness.* Secaucus, NJ: Carol Publishing.

Clance, Pauline Rose, & Imes, Suzanne Ament. (Fall 1978). "The Imposter Phenomenon In High Achieving Women Dynamics and Therapeutic Intervention." *Psychotherapy: Theory, Research and Practice*, 15:3, 242.

Clegg, Eileen M., & Swartz, Susan. (1997). *Goodbye Good Girl.* Oakland, CA: New Harbinger Publications, Inc., 3.

Cook, Ellen Piel. (1993). *Women, Relationships, and Power.* Alexandria, VA: American Counseling Assocation.

Costello, Cynthia B., Miles, Shari, & Stone, Anne J. (eds.). (1998). *The American Woman 1999-2000.* New York, NY: WW Norton & Co., Inc., 263.

Curley, Jayme. (1981). *The Balancing Act II.* Chicago, IL: Chicago Review Press.

DeAngelis, Tori. (August 1997). "Stereotypes still stymie female managers." *American Psychological Association Monitor.* 41-42.

Dowling, Collette. (1988). *Perfect Women.* New York, NY: Summit Books.

Elliott, Miriam, & Meltsner, Susan. (1991). *The Perfectionist Predicament.* New York, NY: William Morrow and Company, Inc.

Gaskill, Stephen. (November 1995). "A Solid Investment: Making Full Use of the Nations' Human Capital." *Recommendations of the Federal Glass Ceiling Commission.* Washington, D.C.: U.S. Government Printing Office.

Heilman, Madeline E., Block, Caryn J, & Martell, Richard F. (1995). "Sex Stereotypes: Do They Influence Perceptions of Managers? Gender in the Workplace." *Journal of Social Behavior and Personality*, 10:6, 237-252. Corte Madera, CA: Select Press.

Hellwig, Basia. (November 1991). "Who Succeeds, Who Doesn't." *Working Woman Magazine*, 16, 108-112.

Hendlin, Steven J. *When Good Enough Is Never Enough*. (1992). New York, NY: G.P. Putnam & Sons.

Levenson, H. (1981). "Differentiating among internality, powerful others, and chance." H. Lefcourt (ed.), *Research with the locus of control construct*. New York: NY: Academic Press, 1, 15-59.

Maglin, Nan Bauer & Perry, Donna (eds.). (1996). *Bad Girls / Good Girls: Women, Sex, and Power in the Nineties*. New Brunswick, NJ: Rutgers University Press.

McGrath, Ellen (ed.), Keita, Gwendolyn (ed.), Stickland, Bonnie (ed.), Russo, Nancy (ed.). (1990). Women and Depression. Washington, D.C.: American Psychological Association.

Mindell, Phyllis. (1995). *A Woman's Guide to the Language of Success: Communicating with Confidence and Power*. Paramus, NJ: Prentice Hall, 37.

Paglia, Camille. (1994). *Vamps and Tramps*. New York, NY: Vintage Books, ix.

Powell, Gary N., & Butterfield, D. Anthony. (1994). "Investigating the "Glass Ceiling" Phenomenon: An Empirical Study of Actual Promotions to Top Management." *Academy of Management Journal*, 37:1, 68-86.

Robinson, Bryan E. (1992). *Overdoing It: How To Slow Down and Take Care of Yourself*. Deerfield Beach, FL: Health Communications, Inc.

Rubin, Harriett. (1997). *The PRINCESSA: Machiavelli for Women*. New York, NY: Doubleday, 19.

Scheinholtz, Debra F. (ed.). (1994). *Cracking the Glass Ceiling: Strategies for Success*. New York, NY: Catalyst.

Tannen, Deborah. (1990). *You Just Don't Understand*. New York, NY: Ballantine Books.

Warner, Carolyn. (1992). *The Last Word*. Englewood Cliffs, NJ: Prentice Hall, 93,180.

Chapter 3

Arnold, Chuck. (June 8, 1998). "Chatter-Oprah Winfrey Commencement Address." *People Magazine*, 138.

Costello, Cynthia B., Miles, Shari, & Stone, Anne J. (eds.). (1998). *The American Woman 1999-2000*. New York, NY: WW Norton & Co., Inc., 263.

Dewey, John. (1963). *Experience and Education*. New York, NY: Macmillan Publishing Co., Inc.

Gaskill, Stephen. (November 1995). *"A Solid Investment: Making Full Use of the Nations' Human Capital."* Recommendations of the Federal Glass Ceiling Commission. Washington, D.C.: U.S. Government Printing Office.

Gilberd, Pamela Boucher. (1996). *The Eleven Commandments of Wildly Successful Women*. New York, NY: Macmillan Spectrum.

Glaser, Connie Brown, & Smalley, Barbara Steinberg. (1992). *More Power To You*. New York, NY: Warner Books, Inc.

Helgesen, Sally. (1990). *The Female Advantage*. New York, NY: Doubleday.

Horner, Althea J. (1989). *The Wish for Power and the Fear of Having It*. Northvale, NJ: Jason Aronson, Inc., 15.

Lerner-Robbins, Helene. (1996). *Our Power As Women: The Wisdom and Strategies of Highly Successful Women*. Berkeley, CA: Conari Press, 19.

Lindbergh, Anne Morrow. (1978). *Gift From The Sea*. New York, NY: Vintage Books.

O'Gorman, Patricia. (1994). *Dancing Backwards In High Heels*. Center City, MN: Hazelden Education Materials.

Prokop, Charles K., & Bradley, Laurence A. (ed.). (1981). *Medical Psychology*, New York, NY: Academic Press.

Scheinholtz, Debra F. (ed.). (1994). *Cracking the Glass Ceiling: Strategies for Success*. New York, NY: Catalyst.

Tunick, George. (January/February 1994). "Success: An Insiders Guide." *Executive Female*, 17:82.

Warner, Carolyn. (1992). *The Last Word*. Englewood Cliffs, NJ: Prentice Hall, 4,47,75,263.

Webster, E. Carol. (1993). *Success Management*. Pompano Beach, FL: Printing Corporation of the Americas, Inc.

Wolf, Naomi. (1993). *Fire with Fire: The New Female Power and How To Use It.* New York, NY: Random House, Inc., 238.

Chapter 4

Aburdene, Patricia, & Naisbitt, John. (1992). *Megatrends for Women: From Liberation to Leadership.* New York, NY: Ballantine Books.

Bem, Sandra Lipsitz. (1993). *The Lenses of Gender: Transforming the Debate on Sexual Inequality.* New Haven, CT: Yale University, 130.

Boles, Janet K., & Hoeveler, Diane Long. (1996). *From the Goddess to the Glass Ceiling: A Dictionary of Feminism.* Lanham, MD: Madison Books.

Brody, Jane E. (December 9, 1992). "For the Professional Mother Rewards May Outweigh Stress." *New York Times.*

Chicago Area Partnerships. (1996). *Pathways & Progress: Corporate Best Practices to Shatter the Glass Ceiling.* Chicago, IL, 9.

Conway, Jill K., Bourque, Susan C., & Scott, Joan W. (eds.). (1987). *Learning About Women: Gender, Politics, and Power.* Ann Arbor, MI: The University of Michigan Press.

Costello, Cynthia B., Miles, Shari, & Stone, Anne J. (eds.). (1998). *The American Woman 1999-2000.* New York, NY: WW Norton & Co., Inc., 263.

Costello, Cynthia, & Krimgold, Barbara Kivimae (eds.). (1996). *The American Woman 1996-97: Where We Stand.* New York, NY: W.W. Norton & Co., Inc.

Faludi, Susan. (1992). *Backlash: The Undeclared War Against American Women.* New York, NY: Doubleday.

Friedan, Betty. (1963). *The Feminine Mystique.* New York, NY: W.W. Norton & Co., Inc.

Friedan, Betty. (1997). *Beyond Gender.* Baltimore, MD: The John Hopkins University Press, 6.

Gaskill, Stephen. (November 1995). "A Solid Investment: Making Full Use of the Nations' Human Capital." *Recommendations of the Federal Glass Ceiling Commission.* Washington, D.C.: U.S. Government Printing Office.

Ireland, Patricia (ed.). (Summer 1998). "NOW Takes Action Against Sexual Harassment." *National NOW Times,* 30:3, 1-12.

Kroeger, Brooke. (July 1994). "The Road Less Rewarded." *Working Woman Magazine*, 19:50-55.

Mainiero, Lisa. (Spring 1994). "On Breaking the Glass Ceiling: The Political Seasoning of Powerful Women Executives." *Organizational Dynamics*, 22:4-20.

Miller, Jean Baker. (1986). *toward a new psychology of women*. Boston, MA: Beacon Press, 96.

Morrison, Ann M., White, Randall P., & VanVelsor, Ellen. (1992). *The Center from Creative Leadership: Breaking the Glass Ceiling, Can Women reach the top of America's largest corporations*. Redding, MA: Addison/ Wesley Publishing Company, Inc, 19.

Neft, Naomi, & Levine, Ann D. (1997). *Where Women Stand: An International Report on the Status of Women in 140 Countries* 1997-1998. New York, NY: Random House, Inc.

Powell, Gary N., & Butterfield, D. Anthony. (1994). "Investigating the "Glass Ceiling" Phenomenon: An Empirical Study of Actual Promotions to Top Management." *Academy of Management Journal*, 37,1:68-86.

Read, Phyllis J., & Witlieb, Bernard L. (1992). *The Book of Women's Firsts*. New York, NY: Random House, Inc.

Reddy, Helen. (1972). *I am Woman*. Capital Records, Inc.

Reid-Merritt, Patricia. (1996). *Sister Power: How Phenomenal Black Women are Rising to the Top*. New York, NY: John Wiley & Sons, Inc.

Scheinholtz, Debra F. (ed.). (1994). *Cracking the Glass Ceiling: Strategies for Success*. New York, NY: Catalyst.

Schonfeld, Erick. "A Fissure In The Glass Ceiling." *Fortune Magazine*, 15.

Smeal, Eleanor, & Jackman, Jennifer. (July 28, 1998). "National Women's Equality Act for the 21st Century." Feminist Majority Web Site http://www.feminist.org.

Steinem, Gloria. (1994). *Moving Beyond Words*. New York, NY: Simon & Schuster, Inc.

Stith, Anthony. (1996). *Breaking the Glass Ceiling: Racism and Sexism in Corporate America: The Myth's, The Realities, and The Solutions*. Orange, NJ: Bryant & Dillon Publishers.

Stroh, Linda K., Brett, Jeanne M., & Reilly, Anne H. (1992). "All the Right Stuff: A Comparison of Female and Male Managers Career Progression." *Journal of Applied Psychology*, 77:3, 251-260.

U.S. Department of Labor, Office of Public Affairs. (November 22, 1995). "The Glass Ceiling Commission Unanimously Agrees on 12 Ways to Shatter Barriers." *News Release*, 95-483.

U.S. Department of Labor, Women's Bureau. (September 1996). "Facts on Working Women." *Government Pamphlet*, 96-2.

Walker, Rebecca (ed.). (1995). *to be real*. New York, NY: Doubleday.

Warner, Carolyn. (1992). *The Last Word*. Englewood Cliffs, NJ: Prentice Hall, 99,179.

Wollstonecraft, Mary. (1996). *A Vindication of the Rights of Woman*. Mineola, NY: Dover Publications, Inc.

Chapter 5

Barnett, Rosalind C. (1991). *Research on The Effect of Women's Outside Employment: A Review for Clinical Practitioners*. Wellesley College, Center for Research on Women, Working Papers Series 221.

Barnett, Rosalind C. (1994). *Home-to-Work Spillover Revisited: A Study of Full-Time Employed Women in Dual-Earner Couples*. Wellesley College, Center for Research on Women, Working Papers Series 271.

Bellafante, Ginia. (June 29, 1998). "Feminism: It's All About Me!" *Time Magazine*, 151:25,54-62.

Bem, Sandra Lipsitz. (1975). "Sex Roles Adoptability: One Consequence of Psychological Androgyny." *Journal of Personality and Social Psychology*, 31,4:634-643.

Clegg, Eileen M., & Swartz, Susan. (1997). *Goodbye Good Girl*. Oakland, CA: New Harbinger Publications, Inc.

Costello, Cynthia B., Miles, Shari, & Stone, Anne J. (eds.). (1998). *The American Woman 1999-2000: A Century of Change-What's Next?* New York, NY: WW Norton & Co., Inc., 263.

Costello, Cynthia, & Krimgold, Barbara Kivimae (eds.). (1996). *The American Woman 1996-97: Where We Stand*. New York, NY: W.W. Norton & Co., Inc.

Culotta, Elizabeth. (April 16, 1993). "Entrepreneurs Say: "It's Better to Be the Boss." *Science Magazine*, 406.

Crosby, Faye J. (1991). *Juggling*. New York, NY: The Free Press.

DeAngelis, Tori. (August 1997). "Stereotypes still stymie female managers." *American Psychological Association Monitor*. Public Interest 41-42.

Enns, Carolyn Zerbe. (1997). *Feminist Theories and Feminist Psychotherapies*. Binghamton, NY: The Haworth Press, Inc.

French, Marilyn. (1986). *Beyond Power: On Women, Men, and Morals*. New York, NY: Ballantine Books, 488.

Friedan, Betty. (1997). *Beyond Gender*. Baltimore, MD: The John Hopkins University Press, 6.

Friedan, Betty. (1977). *It Changed My Life*. New York, NY: Dell Publishing Co., Inc.

Glick, P., & Fiske, S.T. (1996) "The Ambivalent Sexism Inventory: Differentiating Hostile and Benevolent Sexism." *Journal of Personality and Social Psychology*, *70*, 491-512.

Ireland, Patricia (ed.). (Summer 1998). "NOW Takes Action Against Sexual Harassment." *National NOW Times*, 30:3, 1-12.

Jordan, Judith V., Kaplan, Alexandra G., Miller, Jean Baker, Stiver, Irene P., Surrey, Janet L. (1991). *Women's Growth and Connection: Writings from the Stone Center*. New York, NY: Guilford Press.

Jordan, Judith V. (ed.). (1997). *Women's Growth in Diversity: More Writings from the Stone Center*. New York, NY: Guilford Press.

Klonis, S., Endo, J., Crosby, F., & Worell, J. (1997). "Feminism As Life Raft". *Psychology of Women Quarterly*, 21, 340.

Lehrman, Karen. (1997). *The Lipstick Proviso: Women, Sex & Power in the Real World*. New York, NY: Doubleday, 35.

Maglin, Nan Bauer & Perry, Donna (eds.). (1996). *Bad Girls / Good Girls: Women, Sex, and Power in the Nineties*. New Brunswick, NJ: Rutgers University Press, xiii.

Neft, Naomi, & Levine, Ann D. (1997). *Where Women Stand: An International Report on the Status of Women in 140 Countries 1997-1998*. New York, NY: Random House, Inc.

Reid-Merritt, Patricia. (1996). *Sister Power: How Phenomenal Black Women are Rising to the Top.* New York, NY: John Wiley & Sons, Inc., 212.

Sommers, Christina Hoff. (1994). *Who Stole Feminism? How Women Have Betrayed Women.* New York, NY: Simon & Schuster.

Tavris, Carol. (1992). *The Mismeasure of Women.* New York, NY: Simon & Schuster.

Twenge, Jean M. (1997) "Attitudes Toward Women, 1970-1995: Meta-Analysis", *Psychology of Women Quarterly, 21,* 35-51.

Walker, Rebecca (ed.). (1995). *to be real.* New York, NY: Doubleday, 215.

Wolf, Naomi. (1993). *Fire with Fire: The New Female Power and How To Use It.* New York, NY: Random House, Inc., 36.

Chapter 6

Bass, Bernard M., & Avolio, Bruce J. (1994). "Shatter the Glass Ceiling: Women May Make Better Managers." *Human Resource Management Periodical,* 33:4, 549-560.

Belenky, Mary Field, Clinchy, Blythe, McVicker, Goldberger, Nancy Rule, Tarule, Jill Mattuck. (1997). *Women's Ways of Knowing. The Development of Self, Voice, and Mind.* New York, NY: BasicBooks, Inc.

Boles, Janet K., & Hoeveler, Diane Long. (1996). *From the Goddess to the Glass Ceiling: A Dictionary of Feminism.* Lanham, MD: Madison Books.

Costello, Cynthia B., Miles, Shari, & Stone, Anne J. (eds.). (1998). *The American Woman 1999-2000.* New York, NY: W. W. Norton & Co., Inc., 263.

Geary, David C. (1998). *Male, Female: The Evolution of Human Sex Differences.* Washington, DC: American Psychological Association.

Gilligan, Carol. (1982). *In a Different Voice: Psychological Theory and Women's Development.* Cambridge, MA: Harvard University Press.

Helgesen, Sally. (1990). *The Female Advantage.* New York, NY: Doubleday.

Hendricks, Bill. (November 13, 1994). "Do Women Top Men in Brain Power?" *The Atlanta Journal.*

Hendricks, Bill. (November 13, 1994). "Separate but equal: The sexes match in IQ, but females have more." *The Atlanta Journal.*

Horchler, Joane Nelson. (November 5, 1990). "When She's the Man for the Top Job." *Industry Week*, 239, 47-48.

Jordan, Judith V., Kaplan, Alexandra G., Miller, Jean Baker, Stiver, Irene P., Surrey, Janet L. (1991). *Women's Growth and Connection: Writings from the Stone Center.* New York, NY: Guilford Press.

Jordan, Judith V. (ed.). (1997). *Women's Growth in Diversity: More Writings from the Stone Center.* New York, NY: Guilford Press.

Lindbergh, Anne Morrow. (1978). *Gift From The Sea.* New York, NY: Vintage Books, 26.

Lorber, Judith. (1994). *Paradoxes of Gender.* New Haven, CT: Yale University Press.

McAllen, Jack. (1993). *The Boss Should Be A Woman.* Nevada City, CA: Blue Dolphin Publishing.

Miller, Jean Baker. (1986). *toward a new psychology of women.* Boston, MA: Beacon Press.

Moir, Anne & Jessel, David. (1989). *Brain Sex: The Real Differences Between Men and Women.* New York, NY: Dell Publishing, 7.

Moskal, Brian S. (April 18, 1994). "Glass Ceiling, Beware!" *Industry Week*, 13-14.

Neft, Naomi, & Levine, Ann D. (1997). *Where Women Stand: An International Report on the Status of Women in 140 Countries 1997-1998.* New York, NY: Random House, Inc.

Rosener, Judy B. (1995). *America's Competitive Secret: Women Managers.* New York, NY: Oxford University Press.

Scheinholtz, Debra F. (ed.). (1994). *Cracking the Glass Ceiling: Strategies for Success.* New York, NY: Catalyst, 21.

Stephens, Autumn. (1996). *Wild Words from Wild Women.* Berkeley, CA: Conari Press, 166.

Tannen, Deborah. (1994). *Talking from 9 to 5: Women and Men in the Workplace: Language, Sex and Power.* New York, NY: Avon Books.

Zahniser, J.D. (ed.). (1989). *And Then She Said.* Port Murray, NJ: Calleich Press, 58.

Chapter 7

Cantor, Dorothy W., & Bernay, Toni. (1992). *Women in Power: The Secrets of Leadership.* New York, NY: Houghton Mifflin Company, 49.

Costello, Cynthia, & Krimgold, Barbara Kivimae (eds.). (1996). *The American Woman 1996-97: Where We Stand.* New York, NY: W.W. Norton & Co., Inc.

Costello, Cynthia B., Miles, Shari, & Stone, Anne J. (eds.). (1998). *The American Woman 1999-2000.* New York, NY: WW Norton & Co., Inc., 263.

Donovan, Patrick. (November 24, 1997). "Nurturing women in the world of business. Melbourne, Australia: The Age Melbourne Online, http://www.theage.com.au/daily/971124/bus/bus11.html.

Feminist.com. (1998). "Third Wave Foundation." Feminist.com Web Site http://www.feminist.com.

Friedan, Betty. (1997). *Beyond Gender.* Baltimore, MD: The John Hopkins University Press, 6.

Kauffman-Rosen, Leslie. (March 27, 1995). "Holes in the Glass Ceiling Theory." *Newsweek,* 125, 24-25.

Maglin, Nan Bauer & Perry, Donna (eds.). (1996). *Bad Girls / Good Girls: Women, Sex, and Power in the Nineties.* New Brunswick, NJ: Rutgers University Press.

National Foundation for Women Business Owners. (March 27, 1996). "Women Owned Businesses in the United States." National Foundation for Women Business Owners Web Site http://www.nfwbo.org

Neft, Naomi, & Levine, Ann D. (1997). *Where Women Stand: An International Report on the Status of Women in 140 Countries 1997–1998.* New York, NY: Random House, Inc.

Orlando Sentinel, The. (July 25, 1998). "Gearing up for a global 'girl power' revolution." Associated Press, C-1.

Paludi, M. (1987). Psychometric Properties and underlying assumptions of four objective measures of fear of success. In M. Walsh (Ed.) *The psychology of women,* 185-202. New Haven, CT: Yale University Press.

Peplau, L. (1976). Impact of fear of success and sex-role attitudes on women's competitive achievement. *Journal of Personality and Social Psychology*, 34:4, 561-568.

Pfost, K. and Fiore, M. (1990). Pursuit of non-traditional occupations: Fear of success or fear of not being chosen? *Sex-roles*, 23:1-2, 15-24.

Scheinholtz, Debra F. (ed.). (1994). *Cracking the Glass Ceiling: Strategies for Success.* New York, NY: Catalyst, 20.

Skorneck, Carolyn. (October 1, 1998). "First ladies rally 'round Hillary Clinton." *Sun Sentinel.* Fl.: Associated Press.

Smith, Nancy DuVergne,. (Spring-Summer 1998). "Girls and Boys Making Connections Through the Gender Relation Project." *Memberlink*, Newsletter for members of the Wellesley Centers for Women.

Sommers, Christina Hoff. (1994). *Who Stole Feminism? How Women Have Betrayed Women.* New York, NY: Simon & Schuster, 246.

Symposium on Women in the Enterprise. (March 9, 1996). Website: http://athensnews.dolnet.gr.

Warner, Carolyn. (1992). *The Last Word.* Englewood Cliffs, NJ: Prentice Hall, 178.

Wiltz, Theresa. (May 1991). "Glass Ceiling Survival." *Essence Magazine*, 22:35-37.

Witt, Linda, Paget, Karen M., & Matthews, Glenna. (1994). *Running As A Woman: Gender and Power in American Politics.* New York, NY: The Free Press.

Deliver the Dream

Our ability to strike a balance—between work and family, between feminine and masculine talents, between our own well-being and our responsibilities to others, in virtually all aspects of our lives—is a power message that is interwoven throughout the stories presented in this book. As women have attempted to manage this struggle, they've given rise to the newest frontier for successful businesswomen, exploring philanthropy. Philanthropy allows us, as women, to take the success we've achieved and share that success with those less fortunate. By giving, we stay centered and grounded, and by remembering those still struggling to find their positive power, we can foster even greater personal development and fulfillment as we seek balance for ourselves.

Now that many women are learning to rise above the Glass Ceiling and dance on it, we need to ascend to the next step and show our strengths and power in the world of philanthropy. This drive for women to give back to the community has been named *FEMALETHINK* by researchers. I've witnessed the rise to this next level first hand in someone I personally respect and admire. Pat Moran, President and CEO of JM Family Enterprises, Inc., and author of this book's foreword has tapped danced across the beams of the Glass Ceiling and now is taking strides to fulfill her need and further find her own personal balance by giving back to the community.

Pat shared a vision to develop a beautiful mountainous retreat where children, families and individuals recovering from illness or life crisis could come. A place where those in need could relax and refocus their lives. A place where guiding, directional support is given in a nurturing environment. A place where horseback riding, marshmallow roasting and raft races across the lake overshadow the experiences that lead them to the retreat in the first place. Pat shared her dream and was met with overwhelming enthusiasm by her peers, colleagues and myself. Deliver the Dream, Inc. will have a grand opening in the year 2000. The site selected is Laurel Falls, a mountain retreat and enrichment center providing directional support, recreation and relaxation for children, families and individuals in need. Deliver the Dream, Inc. is overseen by a board of business professionals who are making Pat's personal dream of strengthening families and helping people regain their personal and emotional power will now be realized.

I've seen the dedication of Pat's staff and know of her personal involvement in ensuring the direction and mission of the retreat is achieved. The true fulfillment of Pat's dream will be realized for many years to come as each person visits and benefits from its existence. Endorsed by Ronald McDonald House Charities, Deliver the Dream, Inc. hopes to win the endorsement of all those who gain knowledge of its mission. Part of my dream is women-to-women networking, activating our personal dreams and the dreams of the community, weaving positive power bonds and changing the fabric of society. Deliver the Dream, Inc. is a step on the road to a more nurturing society.

For more information . . .

Deliver the Dream, Inc.
PO Box 4077
Deerfield Beach, Florida 33442-4077
1-888-OURDREAM (687-3732)

INDEX

A

Act for Better Childcare, 148
Addams, Jane, 139
Affirmations, 44, 101, 104, 107, 110, 113, 116, 119, 123, 127, 130
Affirmative action, 151
Albright, Madeline, 208
Alliances, 96, 114, 115, 116, 127, 130, 131
Andrews, Lyn D., 21
Androcentrism, 28, 52, 96, 182
Androgyny, 168, 169
Anthony, Susan B., 138
Anti-beauty, 165
Anti-Family, 167
Anti-male, 159
Arnold, Amy, 57
Assertiveness training, 28
Attractiveness, 26, 166

B

Bader-Ginsburg, Ruth, 208
Baker-Miller, Jean, 150
Balance, 13, 188, 189
Barnett, Rosalyn, 167
Bem, Sandra, 52, 133, 144
Bitch perception, 82, 101, 124
Brain structure, 181
Brody, Jane E., 147
Brown, Corrine, 132
Bunker, Edith, 82
Business Matrix, 199

C

Cady-Stanton, Elizabeth, 137
Capocci, Belisario, 197
Capital Across America, 207

Catalyst, 45, 203, 192
Center for Creative Leadership, 153
Change agent, 82, 119, 124, 125, 126
Change tolerant, 179
Chicago Area Partnership, 151
Clinton, Hillary Rodham, 201
Collaboration, 186
Commission on the Status of Women, 138, 140
Competencies, 60, 61, 106, 128, 129, 130, 131
Conflict, 30, 43, 47, 64, 65, 66, 67, 81, 82, 83
Congressional Congress for Women's Issues 140
Corpus callosum, 183
Counter thoughts, 44, 55, 59, 63, 66, 71, 74, 77, 80, 83, 86, 94
Creativity, 191, 197

D

Data gatherers, 183, 184
Day-O'Connor, Sandra, 208
Dewey, John, 102
Dilke, Dame Emilia, 41
Diversity, 148, 149, 158, 159, 171, 176, 183, 186, 202
Divisiveness, 199
Double-speak, 70

E

Empowerment, 149, 191
Endorphins, 26, 121
Equal Employment Opportunity Commission, 142
Equal Pay Act, 140
Equal Rights Advocates, 150

Equal Rights Amendment, 143

F
Faludi, Susan, 143
Family and Medical Leave Act, 148
Federal Glass Ceiling Commission, 36, 151, 152
Female behaviors, 23, 49
Female Think, 191
Femininity, 27
Feminism, history of, 137-150
Feminism, renewed, 157-177, 212
Ferraro, Geraldine, 208
First Wave, 137, 138, 139, 212
French, Marilyn, 170
Freud, Anna, 93
Friedan, Betty, 136, 140, 144, 161, 170
Fukuda-Parr, Sakiko, 208

G
Gender characteristics, 23, 85
Gender differences, 17, 76, 147, 151
Gender equity, 144
Gender lenses, 52
Gender stereotypes, 28, 45, 49, 76
Gender war, 161, 162
Genderlects, 164
Gender-neutral, 168
Giertz, Holly, 125, 126, 127, 212, 213, 214, 215, 216
Glass Ceiling, 36, 37, 39, 44, 45, 46, 66, 92, 125, 127, 139, 151, 152, 153, 154, 183, 202, 211, 212, 214

Goddess Movement, 181
Gordon-Brown, Laurie, 81
Grabowski, Linda, 64
Gund, Kathryn, 148

H
Healthy selfish behavior, 99, 100, 101
Hellegson, Sally, 97
Horner, Althea, 130

I
Immune system, 26, 39
Information Sharers, 184
Inner-other focus, 17, 61, 111
Innovators, 191
Integrators, 192
International Women's Day, 138
International Women's Rights Conference, 138
Intuition, women's, 183

J
JM Family Enterprises, 125, 126, 127

K
Kirkpatrick, Jean, 208
Kunin, Madeline, 198

L
Leadership, 190, 191
League of Women Voter, 200
Lesbianism, 160
Lettman, Andrea, 78
Levenson, Hanna, 87
Lindbergh, Anne Morrow, 188

M

Martin, Dawn, 148
Misandrism, 159
Misogyny, 159
Mistake, 35, 36, 56, 57, 58, 59
Moir and Jessel, 182, 198
Moran, Pat, 13, 14, 125, 173
Morley-Martin, Lynn, 151
Mott, Lucretia, 137
MS, 145
Multitask Wizards, 188

N

National Organization for
    Women, 140, 148
National Women's Equality Act,
    149
National Women's Political
    Caucus, 140
Negative images, 24, 30
Neuter, 168
Novello, Antonia, 208
NOW, See National
    Organization for Women
Nurturing, 65, 168, 176

O

O'Connor, Sandra Day, 145
Offerman, Lynn, 24, 31
Other-focus, 17, 61, 111

P

Paglia, Camelia, 82
Paludi, Michele A., 198
Partnership, 198
Pelosi, Nancy, 201
People pleaser, 50, 51, 54, 55
Perfectionism, 58, 59

Pfost and Fury, 198
Pink collar, 142
Positive power, 32, 47, 160
Power, 21-39, 43-47, 130
Power blocks, 25
Power drain, 35, 73, 82, 95, 162,
    177
Power lessons, 95-131
Power robber, 43-92
Power Sharers, 186
Power stigma, 30
Power, defined, 24, 25
Power, positive lessons, 47, 93
Psychological test, 88

R

Reddy, Helen, 141
Relationships, 26, 62, 63, 108,
    114
Reno, Janet, 208
Richards, Amy, 148
Richards, Heidi, 72
Ride, Sally, 208
Roosevelt, Eleanor, 123
Rudd, Carol, 75

S

Salary differentials, 208
Sanger, Margaret, 139
Santini, Terry, 53
Schroeder, Pat, 49
Second Wave, 48, 141-147, 168
Self-talk, 98, 120, 121, 122, 123,
    129
Seneca Falls, 138, 149
Seneca Falls Convention, 138
Shelley, Mary Wollstonecraft, 137
Sisterhood, 171, 172, 173